Cut The Crap

and **WRITE THAT DAMN SCREENPLAY!**

by

Nicholas Iandolo

Published in the United States by Lulu.com

ISBN: 978-0-557-53728-0

Cover design by Susan Howland (my illustrious super wife). Friends who appear on the cover: Krystle Kelly (front cover); Peter K. Fogarty (back cover bottom); and Joseph V. Mullin, MBA/TM (back cover top)—thanks everyone for allowing this lunatic (yours truly) to tell all of you to "Cut the crap and write that damn screenplay!" And a special thank you to Ali Koushan, proprietor of the Paradise Café (Dedham, MA)—part of his awesome café appears on the front cover of this book and this is where I wrote the damn thing.

Printed in the United States of America

Visit *www.tenthsphere.com* for updates to this book as well as related events and announcements.

First Edition

eBook version available.

This book is wholly dedicated to my spectacularly wonderful wife, Sue. Without her selfless support and encouragement, any success in my writing endeavors would not be possible. She is my love, my partner in all aspects of my life, and my beacon of light that sweeps away all fears and self-consciousness.

ACKNOWLEDGMENTS

I would like to thank my best friend, writer, and filmmaker, Daniel G. Thron (*Hol, Suck, Spoiler*), for his support, encouragement, and invaluable feedback throughout this entire writing process. It was Dan who suggested that I write a no-bullshit book about getting people off their asses to write. Dan's encyclopedic knowledge of movies and books was a treasure trove of insight from which dozens of books could have resulted.

I also want to thank my other friends for being inspirations to me in one way or another. David C. Bryant (VFX Supervisor, Zoic Studios; *CSI, V, 2012*)—we were UMass Amherst graduating classmates of 1991. Back in school, we knocked out several *Star Trek: The Next Generation* stories and have been giving each other inspiration to write ever since. Gareth Hinds (Graphic Novelist, *Beowulf, King Lear, The Merchant of Venice, The Odyssey*)—no one gets work done like this man. He is an artist extraordinaire. He serves as an example for all of us to follow. I only wish I could keep up with him. Benjamin Hansford (Director, *Tron Rebooted*)—a father like me who channels the love and energy of his son into creating the good work. Just like my beloved daughter does for me, Ben's son helps him to attain his dreams. A parent should always look at life like that. Michael Faradie (Actor, *House M.D., Brotherhood, All My Children*)—though I haven't known Mike for very long his infectious personality was the inspiration for one of my screenplay characters. His youthful energy and "southie" (South Boston) style is a blast to be around and to emulate. Kristin Thalheimer Bingham (My Copyeditor, Co-owner with her husband of *www.deanssweets.com*)—without her tireless efforts to make sense of my madman ravings this book surely would have descended into the abyss of bullshit writing to which I am so opposed. And finally Lincoln L. Redley (composer and musical artist)—my childhood friend who doesn't let me get away with anything less than top quality. His musical perfection serves as the backdrop for my relentless pursuit to write, write often, and write well.

A special nod goes to my buddies Christopher F. Mattera, Ph.D. (Educator and Scholar) and Joel LeFave (Webmaster and Genealogist, owner of *www.pawvillage.com*). It was Chris who turned me on to The Doors; Pink Floyd; The Grateful Dead; Crosby, Stills, and Nash; Bob Dylan; and a shitload of other awesome bands from the sixties and seventies. Furthermore, he also got me into authors such as Whitman, Thoreau, and Hunter S. Thompson to name a few. "Wisdom Hill" baby, "Wisdom Hill." And Joel is my Amiga buddy (as in Commodore's Amiga computer—the finest computer of its day), craft brew beer aficionado, and all-round excellent friend to have in my life. We've won and lost lots of dough together playing craps in Vegas, talked politics and *Battlestar Galactica* (the Ronald D. Moore/David Eick series) for hours on end, and at one time we created eBooks on the Amiga decades before they became a reality.

Furthermore, I want to thank award-winning Lifetime writer and producer Heather Hale; and the late great Blake Snyder, author of the thought-provoking and invigorating *Cat Nation* series of screenwriting books, both of whom I met at the 2009 Great American PitchFest in Burbank California. Ms. Hale's personal consultation pushed me out of my comfort zone to write a romantic comedy that has literally changed my life. Blake's book *Save The Cat!*, master class, and best wishes for me were the inspirations for this book, my screenwriting classes, and helping other writers get started.

And a very special thank you goes to my late mother, Patricia Iandolo. Her constant mantra of "always live your dreams" has stayed with me my entire life and is prevalent in this book. Plus, from her is where I get my acerbic wit.

TABLE OF CONTENTS

TABLE OF CONTENTS

Chapter One: What Kind of Writer Do You Want to Be?

Introduction

"Nick, I've got this great idea for a screenplay, really. Can you tell me how to write one?" This is the question I get asked all the time. Once someone finds out that I've written a bunch of screenplays, they think I'm going to tell them the magical secret to screenwriting so they too can *bang* one out. Well it ain't that easy, pal! Screenwriting's a bitch, and you'd better grow a thick hide if you're going to play this game.

I could wax philosophical about the wondrous esoteric process of writing for the screen. Or how movies spark the imagination and inspire the soul. Or that breathing life into characters and your story is like being there at the birth of your beautiful baby daughter (which I was). Etcetera.

But that's all bullshit and does nothing to get you off your lazy ass and at the keyboard writing.

Here's the goddamn truth.

Writing is both a form of soul-enriching pleasure and a tremendous *pain in the ass*! It is unique among all the arts. But nothing is worth shit if it were easy to attain.

Aside from being a writer, I'm an opera fan—my favorite being Giuseppe Verdi's *La Traviata*. The male protagonist, Alfredo, while wooing the so-called "wanton woman," Violetta, sang that love is both "torment and delight." So is writing—and in some ways even more so when it comes to screenwriting.

Unlike prose or a stage play, screenwriting requires an additional level of vision, veracity, and verve. You have only 120 pages (give or take) to make your point and tell a great story. You can't tell it with long drawn out descriptions or thoughts. You can't beat around the bush with endless dialogue and monologues. And you can't tell it without being both economical and intuitive.

That is screenwriting: a maddening and rewarding endeavor. Torment and delight.

And it is not for timid, the feint of heart, the weekend warrior, or the wannabe writer. You either shit or get off the pot as my late mother used to say. So sit down and write that goddamn story— or you can go to parties and bullshit your friends about how you're a writer who hasn't written *jack*.

Over time, many books have been written on the subject. Books such as Robert McKee's *Story*, Blake Snyder's *Save The Cat!*, and Syd Field's *Screenplay* to name but a few. And many workshops, master classes, private consultations, and screenwriters' conferences are given each year to teach would-be screenwriters this mysterious craft.

And though a neophyte writer should certainly check these out, I say fuck any pretentious nonsense that tells you "not to write."

What do I mean by that? Well, some books would have you spend a ridiculous amount of time trying to establish the value charge of each scene and sequence of scenes; filling out index cards all day long to beat out your scenes; breaking down each character's inner and outer needs and then plotting those needs against each beat of action per scene; writing extensive back stories for each character; drafting 100-page treatments that would result in a 1,000-page screenplay that no one will ever read; charting the story structure to fit pre-determined molds, where certain events happen by certain pages; creating character and action grids, charts, and graphs; and just about every other asinine non-writing exercise you can think of that keeps you from writing your actual story!

Don't get me wrong—there is merit to all of these methods. And their *real value* comes in the revising stage as you boil down and polish your stories into finely tuned scripts that "fly off the page." And if you're an *experienced and established* writer, one or more of these methods are certainly useful when planning your next story. But for the new writer, thinking about having to write hundreds of pages of nonsense before ever writing your screenplay will do nothing but scare the hell out of you and cause you to bag the whole thing.

Or, by the time you finish doing all this so-called *introspective writing*, you end up with months of time spent putzing around pretending to write a screenplay. And what are you left with? A lot of notes and no fucking script.

That's not writing!

That's bullshit.

What good is that?

Writing about the writing you're going to write is not writing.

Writing is writing!

So put down those damn notes, get to the keyboard, and start writing, will ya?

In fact, take my advice here: any book that tells you not to write or to write only in "this way," do the exact opposite.

What would you rather have? A bunch of index cards, a 100-page "unwritable" treatment, all of these nebulous and meaningless charts, or a goddamn screenplay?

Now you're probably saying, "Who is this asshole who thinks he knows better than McKee or Field?"

A guy who decided to stop farting around pretending to write and actually started writing.

A long time ago (not in a galaxy far, far away either), I tried the bullshit "map out the story" method of writing, and I ended up spending more time doing all of the busy work instead of writing the damn story.

I abandoned that project and it took years before I was to give writing a novel another try.

Then one day I decided to say, "Fuck it. I'm writing a novel." And instead of the meticulous wannabe writing method, I went headlong into the story, never, and I mean never, looking back until it was done. And it was done in three months and ten days. Five hundred and thirty-eight pages that didn't exist before. Done motherfucker.

I applied this same method to screenwriting and, lo and behold, the friggin' thing gets done.

Hey, I might not have *War and Peace* on my hands, but I have something that a lot of people wish they had. And you can, too. You only need enough tools to get you started, and I'm going to help you with that—the rest is up to your heart and your balls (metaphorically speaking ladies).

*   *   *

Right now, there are so many screenwriters and screenplays out there that it is literally impossible to produce even a fraction of this cumulative work. Is this a reason *not to write*? Hell no!

Furthermore, there are even more wannabe writers (of every medium) and even more story ideas. So much so that the breadth of this entire so-called canon would dwarf the collected works in the Library of Congress.

And these wannabe writers will never compete with all of those writers who have come before them if they never turn their ideas into a completed work. All of these stories are still floating around in people's heads. Why?

Fear and Self-consciousness.

Writers not only haven't learned the craft well enough to overcome their fear and self-consciousness to start writing and actually finish their work—let alone getting it produced or published—but also lack both the *vision* and the *belief* that they can be writers.

What do I mean by vision and belief?

They are two separate concepts.

- Vision is *seeing* yourself doing the thing that you love most.

- Belief is *knowing* that you will be doing the thing you love most.

In this case, we're talking about being a writer.

Without vision and belief, you might as well put this book down right now. If you cannot see yourself as a writer, and believe in yourself as a writer, how are you going to get the so-called "card holders" (producers, agents, publishers, etc.) to do likewise?

I can't help you if you don't have the talent. I can't help you if you don't have the desire in your heart to write. And I can't help you if you don't have the discipline to write. But I can help you get started, that's where this book comes in.

What Is a "Writable" Story?

As we go through this book, I will be providing you with a series of *simple and short* techniques, exercises, and strategies to help you get your story up and running as quickly as possible—avoiding many of the roadblocks that plague new screenwriters.

Furthermore, these concepts are transferable from screenwriting to novel writing to marketing and communications writing. They are ubiquitous ideas that have helped me write both creatively and for business. Once you understand the principles behind them, you can apply them to all types of publications and media.

Here's where you begin:

You have an idea for a screenplay, but you cannot seem to make a "writable" story out of it. That's where you take the time to learn the craft of writing from a 20,000-foot view level. This is a direct contradiction of what a lot of books on screenwriting will promote.

Writable does not mean marketable, or to be entertainment-industry specific, "high-concept." High-concept is the term that gets thrown around a lot in Hollywood these days regarding movies that have huge earning potential. These stories may even be good but more often than not, they're simply popular cash cows. Some examples of high-concept are *Die Hard, Lethal Weapon, The Notebook, Confessions of a Shopaholic, Sex and the City: The Movie, 1941, Transformers: The Movie, 3:10 to Yuma, The Passion of The Christ*, etcetera. You get the idea.

If you're setting out to write a high-concept movie, then at least make it a good one.

A writable story is one that you (as the writer) can see through to the end. You know your characters, you know the major and minor turning points, you know your overall plot and structure, you have the genre, logline, and title worked out, and you are confident—no chomping at the bit—that you can write this thing and nothing's stopping you.

Not this time, baby!

That's a "writable" story.

Bullshit Writers

Developing a story can be a daunting task. Many times, new writers give up trying to take their story from concept to page. There are many reasons why this happens (such as too much writing about the writing you're going to write). But more often than not, writers invariably fall into writing-like traps, turning them into *bullshit writers,* resulting in never getting to either *FADE IN:* or *FADE OUT:*.

So let's take a few moments to talk about these bullshit writers and see if any of these types apply to you.

There are five types (in reverse-order of the amount of writing they actually get done):

- The Reviser
- The Planner
- The Start-Stopper
- The Thinker
- The Talker

First up are *The Reviser* and *The Planner,* who are more or less on the same level. However, sometimes The Reviser has written more stuff and sometimes The Planner has. The important thing to remember is that neither can get past their initial writing.

The Reviser, having actually written some material, is usually never near completion or cannot for the life of them move on from whatever they've already done. Revisers may never get passed the first few pages, first act, or even less likely, the first draft of their screenplays without going over what they've done again and again, tweaking and changing endlessly.

The problem with revisers is not that they are writing new drafts of their screenplays—revising is a vital part of the screenwriting process—but when The Reviser starts getting into drafts 15, 20, 30, and so on, then it is time to move on. Certainly some of the greatest screenplays have gone through numerous drafts, but this was at a point when the story was fully *developed, sold,* and the *production was well under way,* necessitating many changes.

That's not you.

You, the new screenwriter, do not have the luxury of 20 or more drafts. You should be able to say everything that you need to say in five to seven drafts (sometimes a little more, sometimes a little less) and then get started on your next project. If you don't do this and you are stuck on your first and only screenplay, then when a producer asks you what else you've got and you have nothing else, you're going to feel pretty shitty. Guess you should have stopped at draft seven and started working on that other great idea you had.

More often than not, Revisers are usually stuck on one or more sections of their stories and can't move on because they think it is not perfect enough. Well news flash buddy, it's never going to be perfect enough no matter what you do. At some point, you have to learn to let it go and let the story stand on its own.

If you can't do this with your story, you're not a real writer yet.

Next up is *The Planner*. The Planner spends an enormous amount of time planning and plotting and preparing their story without ever writing one word of the story proper—like what those grandiose screenwriting books will tell you to do. Planners have been known to write pages and pages of story treatments, outlines, synopses, background stories, and just about anything else they can think of, but never one damn word of the actual screenplay.

Don't get me wrong—there is certainly something to be said for doing a goodly amount of research and development for your story and characters, but when it becomes a crutch or an impediment that keeps you from writing FADE IN: and then the rest, you have to stop planning and start writing. Period.

Surprisingly, screenplays can be well-written with modest planning up front. *Casablanca*, for example. The writers were literally writing the script as filming progressed to the very end. Yet, *Casablanca* is considered one of the greatest screenplays ever written.

The key here is to have all of the necessary components of your story in place first and let the process take care of itself. You need to write that first draft in whatever poor form it may be in order to then use the revision process to work out all the bugs and refine the story. And that's where the revered screenwriting books will be your trusty companions on that journey.

All the research in the world won't replace a great story, and Planners are notorious for believing the reverse is true.

The Start-Stopper is a person that is never satisfied with their work. They either put down what they're working on indefinitely (moving on to something else that they think is better), or they keep putting down and picking up their original work while never finishing it.

The Start-Stopper never gets past any significant amount of writing because they are easily distracted and cannot focus. This is often a result of not being able to craft a "writable" story from their great ideas, of which they seem to have many, and so they lose the passion for the work—a death knell to any writer.

Fear and self-consciousness can also turn a potentially great writer into a Start-Stopper. Ninety percent of why people fail at noble endeavors in life is due to fear and self-consciousness. Don't let that be you. Be strong and confident and know you have friends out there that'll help—including me right here.

The Thinker spends most of their time thinking about writing a screenplay but doesn't seem to have the will or courage to take on the task. For whatever reason, they cannot put pen to paper or finger to keyboard and start writing. Thinkers will plot and plan out every aspect of their stories, from individual scenes to full-on dialogue, but keep it all in their heads. They may or may not have told anyone about their story ideas. Regardless, they are too intimidated by the process to sit down and start writing. Fear and self-consciousness also holds back the thinker—and it is that which must be overcome first.

How is it overcome? By arming The Thinker with the solid tools necessary to get the job done—tools such as genre, loglines, titles, and other story development techniques that will embolden The Thinker to rise above their inhibitions and start writing.

Finally, we get to my personal favorite: *The Talker*. I have been this many times. Talkers are famous for telling everyone how much they are going to write this badass script, based on this badass idea, and it is going to rock. Talkers talk about writing stories so much that they spend most of their time talking about writing while never writing a single sentence.

Again, I think that The Talker's problem comes from a fear of doing the actual writing. Just like in any other social or professional situation, Talkers use talking as a crutch to appease their self-conscious desires for acceptance and never produce anything substantial.

Furthermore, Talkers also like to complain about how "hard it is" to write a screenplay. Well, if you want to sit around all day and watch porn, then that's fine by me. But don't tell me how difficult writing a script is when you haven't even written one goddamn word!

Boo hoo. Grow a pair!

Talkers bitch and moan about the amount of work they'd have to put into the actual writing, coming up with every excuse under the sun why they can't write today.

There is no pill for laziness. Talkers are their own worst enemies.

Nothing is worth a damn unless you bust your ass to earn it. Period!

Queen Gertrude in Shakespeare's *Hamlet* said it best to Polonius "more matter, less art."

Talkers have to shut the fuck up and start writing. They can do this when they realize that their story, for good or for ill, needs their help to come to life in more than just the transitory sounds of their bullshit rants. Armed with the right tools and a good kick-in-the-ass, The Talker can do just that.

So there you have it: the five bullshit writers and their issues. These people can't get out of their own way in order to get the writing done. Therefore, I'm going to help each of them as best as I can with this book.

Bear in mind that, at one point or another, we have all been one or more of these types. I've been them all!

The key is to identify when you are being one and which one you are being, and then take the necessary actions to correct the problem.

So how do we do that?

We create a "writable" story, fire up the writing passion, bust-ass, kick-ass, and don't look back, that's how!

So what kind of a writer do you want to be? A person who *pretends* to write or a real goddamn writer?

If the latter, then put this fucking book down, get your ass to the keyboard, and start writing!

Don't worry about details, characters, plot, formatting, and all that other stuff.

Succinctly write out your ideas (on the computer or on paper)—whatever you think is relevant to get the writing juices flowing. Don't worry about the form right now. We'll get to all of that soon enough.

You need to get out of your own way and start writing. Now!

When you need help, I'll be here.

Then we'll begin with *genre*.

Chapter Two: Genre

The Rules of the Game

So you've decided to be an actual writer after all. Good for you! You've stopped farting around and you're writing your ass off. Now I'll help you out.

All movies conform to one or more styles/settings called *genre*. The actual definition of genre in literary works is: a category of artistic composition, as in music or literature, characterized by similarities in form, style, or subject matter.

In film, genre is especially important because knowing the genre beforehand can help the new screenwriter get a handle on how their story is going to play out. What I mean by that is that there are *rules of genre* that lend themselves to better and more efficient story development.

We're going to look at several of the most popular genres being represented in motion pictures today and discuss their overarching rules.

Let's name the big ones shall we?

- Drama [*Kramer vs. Kramer, Ordinary People, The Godfather*]

- Comedy [*What About Bob?, Used Cars, Happy Gilmore*]

- Action/Adventure [*Raiders of the Lost Ark, National Treasure*]

- Science Fiction [*Avatar, Alien, Blade Runner, Star Wars*]

- Western [*Unforgiven, Dances with Wolves*]

- Romance [*The Time Traveler's Wife, The Notebook*]

- Thriller [*Edge of Darkness, North by Northwest*]

- Horror [*Friday the 13th, Dawn of the Dead*]

- Mystery [*Three Days of the Condor, Clue, Murder by Decree*]

- Crime [*Seven, Heat*]

- War [*Gettysburg, The Patriot, Saving Private Ryan*]

- Memoir [*Platoon, What's Eating Gilbert Grape?, My Sister's Keeper*]

- Musical [*Moulin Rouge! (2001), Mama Mia*]

- Spiritual/Inspirational [*City of Joy, What Dreams May Come*]

- Maturation/Coming of Age [*The Outsiders, Juno*]

- Film Noir [*The Maltese Falcon, Sunset Boulevard*]

And there are many more. However, more often than not, most movies are a genre hybrid of two or more genres. Movies such as:

Ocean's Eleven and *Fight Club* are straight-up drama comedies or dramedies. *Fight Club* is also a memoir.

Annie Hall, Confessions of a Shopaholic, My Best Friend's Wedding fall into the romantic-comedy class with varying degrees of romance versus comedy.

Star Wars could be considered a sci-fi Western in the vein of *The Magnificent Seven*.

Murder mystery thrillers such as *Chinatown* (also a drama), *Body Heat*, and everyone's favorite, *Basic Instinct,* are seminal works that have kept audiences on the edge of their seats for decades.

And who can forget the musical horrors or *The Rocky Horror Picture Show* and *Phantom of the Paradise*? Their tunes are still hummed on the lips of theatergoers years later.

And one of the more intricate and hard to write genre hybrids is the memoir thriller. *American Psycho* and *Good Fellas* fall into this unique slot. They could also be considered crime dramas.

The salient point here is to *know your story's genre* before you start writing it. The reason for this is that once you have an idea as to what type of story you are going to write, you can then figure out the "rules of the game" for that story.

Now I use the term "rules of the game" rather loosely, as there are truly no hard and fast rules for writing in a particular genre. However, it does help to know what the tenets are of a genre or a genre hybrid so that you will have a clearer and more focused image in your head as to what you're writing.

For example, say you were setting out to write a romantic comedy. The general guidelines for a "rom-com" (as it is commonly referred to) are: boy meets girl, boy loses girl, the world around boy and girl haphazardly falls apart, a series of comedic hijinks will usually right the world, boy and girl reconcile, and the antagonist gets theirs in the end.

So keeping those concepts in mind, would you write a rom-com that had: a murder, a war between two rival groups or communities, boy and girl kept apart by religion or social class, etcetera?

Of course not.

You are not writing *Romeo and Juliet* as a romantic comedy. And you wouldn't write *Star Wars* as a crime story. Nor would you consider *The Godfather* an inspirational tome—unless you are fixing to enter into the criminal underworld as a career. Then perhaps you might want to watch *Good Fellas* to catch a glimpse of your possible fate.

Therefore, know the rules of the genre or genre hybrid and then plan out your story accordingly.

How do you determine the rules?

Well that's very simple. WATCH MOVIES.

You can quickly get up to speed on a genre's rules by watching the very movies set in them.

For example, watch *Casablanca* and you'll see how a romance generally works. Long lost lovers reunite, the love is usually doomed from the start, a sacrifice must be made to preserve the memory of the love the protagonists once shared.

As Bogie said to Bergman at the end of *Casablanca* letting her go on a plane to America with her husband "we'll always have Paris."

Science fiction (sci-fi for short) genre films can and indeed get very complicated despite their deceptively simplistic overtones. *Blade Runner,* for example, is both a sci-fi story but also a crime drama with underpinnings of film noir and (depending on what version you watch) a memoir.

Sci-fi stories generally have several common themes. First and foremost is *science.* But more importantly, science fiction is about how science and technology affects people's lives for good or for ill. Usually for ill, which is what makes up a good sci-fi story.

Also sci-fi tends to be "introspective" for one or more characters, despite the ostensible space battles or over-the-top action sequences that characterize many sci-fi movies—though not a requirement for good sci-fi.

The characters are caught in a world where science and technology has overrun the human spirit. They are usually pondering how they got to this point, their ultimate fate, and what they can do about it.

Alien, The Terminator, The Matrix, Silent Running, and Avatar, to name a few, have very introspective characters from Ellen Ripley to Neo to Jake Sully.

Let's look at one more genre, shall we? The Western.

Westerns are great for story telling and are very easy to devise the rules. For example, in a Western, you have a protagonist who is usually a lone gunslinger or a brooding recluse with a past. You have a well-established antagonist like the "head of the town de facto kingpin," whose sole mission is to make life a living hell for the protagonist. Westerns are usually set in the old American West circa the late 1800s.

However, this is not always the case.

Outland, starring Sean Connery, set on a mining colony on one of Jupiter's moons may ostensibly be a sci-fi genre film, but at its heart, it is truly a Western.

Connery is the new sheriff in town, having to deal with the local overlord of the colony, played by Peter Boyle. There's lots of murder, crime, tension, and eventually a showdown that is not unlike the classic Western gunfight.

And to that point, Westerns have gunfights and showdowns, drinking at the saloon, gambling, whoring, and just about any other cliché that you can think of. The trick is to make your Western original and avoid cliché as much as possible while paying homage to the classic Western style.

My job here is not to list off every single possible genre, genre hybrid, and all their associated rules. It is to give you an idea of where and how to begin your journey into genre.

You have to do the research yourself and learn as much as you can (within reason) about the genre that you want to write in. Once that is accomplished, we can move on to chiseling the story itching to get out of you, starting with the powerhouse *logline* and a kick-ass *title*.

Chapter Three: Loglines and Titles

Loglines: Your Script's Powerhouse, Baby!

So what's a *powerhouse logline* anyway? Loglines are like knocks at the door to a producer when pitching your screenplay. They are a one- or two-sentence summation of what your story is about. They are the hook, packed with power, that gets the reader to want to ask you more about your story. And they are a great tool to focus your writing, like a laser beam guiding you in the right direction.

Conventional wisdom usually dictates that you write the screenplay first and then put together the logline, tagline, and sometimes a synopsis or treatment. I believe the other way around is a far better way to apply these tools to help your writing along. You can always change or modify them as your writing evolves—as it invariably will.

Let's take a closer look at loglines.

Think of the *TV Guide* description of a movie that tries to hook the viewer into watching. They're either really good or mediocre. That's fine for *TV Guide,* but when you're trying to get a producer or an agent to read your script, you cannot afford a mediocre logline. Your logline must be a *powerhouse* of intrigue that sells the story for you!

Loglines have to convey a sense of irony. A *what if* logline has to be both ironic and almost answer it's own question.

For example: What if you had to relive the same day over and over again? *Groundhog Day*

Certainly, the premise is ironic as you would go crazy having things turn out the opposite of what you intend day after day. Also, you get a sense that this is going to be a bumpy road for the protagonist as they try to solve this unique dilemma.

Here's another one: A man-eating shark terrorizes a sleepy Cape Cod island. *Jaws*

Pretty straightforward, ha? Ironic as sharks don't tend to terrorize people, on an island, that far north. And once the shark really gets going, the islanders certainly *wake up* from their ennui.

How about this one? Can you guess the movie?

A stranded alien needs a little boy's help to find his way home.

That's easy, right? *ET: The Extraterrestrial*

Now that you have an idea of what a logline is, let's take a moment and discuss the differences between *plot, subplot, theme, story concept, story idea, tagline,* and the *logline.*

All of these story elements have something in common: the telling of the story in one form or another.

Plot is the series of main or significant events in a story. *The Maltese Falcon,* for example, has an intriguing plot to say the least:

- Bogie (Humphrey Bogart) as Sam Spade, a private detective, is hired by a mysterious woman (Brigid O'Shaughnessy) to tail an unseen character that purportedly has run off with her sister.

- Bogie's partner is killed during the investigation.

- Bogie is accosted by Cairo (Peter Lorre), who is looking for the famed Maltese Falcon—a bird statuette covered in priceless jewels.

- Bogie makes deals with all the players in search of the bird while trying to keep the police from arresting him for the murder of his partner, and other murders. He even gets romantically involved with Brigid.

- Bogie meets Gutman, the guy behind the murders. He's been searching for the falcon for 17 years.

- Gutman tries to deal with Bogie and double-cross him at the same time in an effort to get the bird.

- Bogie comes into possession of the falcon and keeps it safe while playing all sides against each other.

- Gutman, Cairo, Brigid, and a henchman all show up at Bogie's place. The exchange for the falcon will happen there. There's lots of double-dealing as Bogie tries to keep himself from getting screwed over.

- The Maltese Falcon is delivered. Everyone is excited. The bird turns out to be a fake. Gutman decides to leave with Cairo in search of the real bird in Istanbul. The henchman escapes but is caught and some of the murders are pinned on him. Brigid is also given over to the police as it turns out that she killed Bogie's partner.

- Bogie is off the hook.

Of course, the plot to this classic is way more involved, but those are the highlights.

A *subplot* is the secondary mini-story (or stories) that either complement or contrast the main story (i.e., the plot). For example, in *The Wizard Of OZ*, not only is the main plot Dorothy going to see the wizard and finding a way to get back home, but her companions are also engaging in their own stories. The cowardly lion is searching for courage, the tin man wants a heart, and the scarecrow wishes he had a brain—all of whom through their actions and choices achieve their goals regardless of the wizard's help.

And let's not forget the Wicked Witch of the West. She's got her own problems to deal with: revenge for her evil sister's death, obsession over those ever-sparkling ruby slippers (kind of Carrie Bradshaw-like from *Sex and the City*), and deep down inside she's looking for love and acceptance (it's hard being an evil witch, you know).

Granted, you wouldn't put that many subplots into your story right out of the gate, but one or two should suffice. In my romantic comedy, *Opportunity Knockout*, I have three subplots happening aside from the main boy-meets-girl yadda yadda plot: corporate competition over a coveted contract, best friends dealing with relationships and employment situations of their own, and the main antagonist getting his in the end.

Subplots are wonderful story-telling tools that have withstood the test of time and can lift a mediocre screenplay up to a thrilling one if done right.

Theme (or *controlling idea* as McKee puts it) is essentially what the story is all about. In *Chinatown* the theme is: evil people can get away with murder or worse because they have power and money. The theme of *Pretty Woman* is, as Richard Gere's character Edward says, "You and I are such similar creatures, Vivian. We both screw people for money." In other words, prostitute or ruthless businessman makes no difference; they're the same. That's the theme, not the ostensible love story.

One more, *Star Wars*: freedom will prevail over tyranny at whatever the cost.

Story concept is the same as your story idea but more on an esoteric level. Say your idea is about a guy who wants to get back with his first love, only to find out that she is over in Iraq as a soldier, so he joins the Army to try to be with her. That's a *story idea*. Not a story, not yet. The story concept is much simpler than that: man tries to reconnect with his lost love.

Some of these terms can be interchangeable at times, but most often, when a producer asks you what's the theme of your story, or what's the basic plot, or what's the concept, you had better have a response and it should be clear and concise.

And finally the *tagline*. This is the one liner (or even just a few words) that you'll see on the movie marquee poster. Examples are:

- In space no one can hear you scream. - *Alien*
- They had a date with fate in Casablanca! - *Casablanca*
- There are three sides to this love story! - *Kramer vs. Kramer*
- You'll never go in the water again! - *Jaws*
- Inside everyone is a frontier waiting to be discovered. - *Dances with Wolves*
- Can love survive a thriving economy? - *Opportunity Knockout*

Taglines are those little quips that people will have in the back of their minds when considering going to see a particular flick. They are also very useful when pitching your screenplays. If the executive you're pitching to likes what they hear, the tagline will stick in their head long after the meeting is over.

How do all of these differ from a logline? Well, the logline uses key parts from all of the above but repackages them into a selling tool. A powerhouse logline hooks the reader (or executive, if you're pitching the story in person) and gets them to want to know more.

Here's the logline from *Opportunity Knockout* that the award-winning Lifetime producer/writer, Heather Hale, helped me develop when I attended the 2009 Great American PitchFest.

> At the top of the dot-com bubble, two executive recruiters who work for rival firms fall in love while competing for a multi-million dollar contract.

Okay, so you get the idea? At this point during my workshops, I do a little exercise with my students. In two-minutes or less, can you sum up your story idea (even though you haven't written it yet) and pitch it?

Being able to concisely and confidently throw your story idea out there to a potential reader (an agent, producer, development executive, etc.) is the hallmark of a good writer. Writers don't just write, they tell stories—emphasis on the *tell*. This is especially true if you're trying to sell your screenplay or get published.

So formulate your thoughts and tell me what your story is all about. The clock starts now!

How did you do?

Let's say you tried to pitch a story about a woman who was jilted at the altar and decides to go on a weekend get-away with her girlfriends.

Okay, that's a good start, but ask yourself where's the hook? What about this story is going to grab the reader and keep them wanting more? And what's the opposition?

You could pitch it like this.

> WEAKEND ADVANCES
>
> A romantic coming-of-age story with a bit of humor thrown in for good measure.
>
> *A naive woman who's been jilted at the altar goes on a weekend get-away. After she arrives, her ex-fiancé shows up with his new girlfriend.*

At this point, hopefully you've hooked the exec enough for them to say, "Tell me more." And no, there is not a typo in the title; it's deliberately spelled that way for a reason that I'll explain later.

Here's the rest of the story:

> SARAH MOORE, a young and naïve admin. assistant dreams of her wedding day. When the day arrives, however, instead of the groom waiting for her at the altar, she is handed a note. She's just been jilted, *old-school.*

Months later, she and her intrepid posse of girlfriends head out to a posh resort in the Hamptons. Just when she starts to settle in and relax, who walks into the hotel but none other than her ex-fiancé with a leggy blonde wrapped on his arm.

Sarah contemplates leaving, but at the urging of her cheering section, she decides enough is enough and stays. Her decision is helped along by the sudden flirtations of a married (but cheating) lothario guest, and her uncontrollable attraction to the genuinely kind-hearted and dapper concierge (who's engaged to be married). This time, Sarah doesn't mind all the attention and behaves way out of character.

What ensues is a duel of peacockery between the lothario (whom Sarah sleeps with right off as a revenge fuck) and Sarah's ex (now regretting jilting this newer sexier Sarah), all the while she's aggressively trying to seduce the concierge. The choices she makes as she deals with each one in turn and in concert evolves her in ways she never dreamed of. Even her friends are shocked by her actions. Ultimately, she finds herself becoming the very thing that she loathes: a home wrecker.

Caught practically mauling the concierge by his fiancée, Sarah has managed to ruin the pending wedding. She also alienates her friends, gets into a knock-down drag-out fist fight with the lothario's wife, and after a drunken escapade of destruction, gets herself kicked out of the hotel.

Sarah hits rock bottom.

Then she finds an unlikely ally in her ex's new girlfriend—now wise to his philandering ways. Together they manage to fix the mess that Sarah caused. They make amends with Sarah's friends, pay for all the damage done to the hotel, and even enlist the help of the lothario's wife (who turns out to actually be a cougar) to get the bride-to-be to forgive her fiancé.

In the end, Sarah is no longer a naïve young lady, as she sends her ex packing and the lothario back to his equally mischievous wife.

In the last scene, we see Sarah and her friends (the ex's girlfriend included) attending the concierge's wedding. A handsome man sits down next to her. He and Sarah make eyes with each other. She says, "Before I ask you your name, do you have a steady girlfriend? Or are you engaged? Or are you married? Oh, and are you straight?" He replies, "'No' to the first three and 'yes' to the last." She smiles at him and says, "Good."

Is that a "writable" story? Yes.

Our logline describes a naïve woman who has to go through some serious shit in order to grow up. Placing her in the unenviable position of having to deal with her ex (and his new girlfriend) in a closed environment such as the resort is a great way to set up tension that carries the story. Furthermore, we add several layers of opposition to spice things up: Sarah dealing with the attentions of two unscrupulous men, Sarah losing herself to become a "home wrecker," ruining the concierge's wedding out of her own insecure desire for revenge, the lothario wife's wrath, and Sarah going off the deep end, getting tossed out of the hotel.

Thanks to the genre, logline, and title (more on titles in the next section), we can see the story heading in this direction. The challenge here is to now write ourselves out of the corner and fix the entertaining disaster that our main character (or *protagonist*— more on that in the next chapter) has caused.

Granted, you may not have the details of your story figured out at this point, but you'll know where you're headed as you continue to write it. Just keep in mind that you're going to make changes as you go along, drop stuff, add stuff, and rework stuff. That's writing.

Let's do another one, shall we? My personal favorite: science fiction.

LITTLE WAR

Sci-fi alien invasion epic adventure and everyman hero story.

Two alien superpowers have their proxy war on Earth, and it is up to us to stop it.

RUSSELL IANELLI was a hard-working American auto service technician. He was a good single father, paid his taxes, and had the respect of his peers—until his daughter was killed by forces beyond his control. Now he's angry, vengeful, and the perfect man to lead a ragtag group of resistance fighters against not one but two alien invading armies.

On the other side of the world is MARIKO MORI, a former Tokyo pop star and actress now turned freedom fighter in the wastelands of China's Kamchatka peninsula (previously a territory of Russia). She's also searching for her sister who was taken by one of the alien armies long ago. A master martial artist (trained for her movie roles), Mariko holds the key to humanity's liberation from alien domination.

Both are fighting for the same goal: kick the aliens off their planet.

Back in 2015, much progress had been made by way of world peace. New technologies had started to reverse centuries of environmental destruction. Global markets blossomed in new industries with the promise of a good job for everybody. And thanks to a series of promising new therapeutic drugs, many diseases that have eternally plagued mankind had been eradicated. But it was all a lie!

The year is now 2025, and much of the Earth has become a bombed-out wasteland where the alien armies and their human collaborators fight a proxy war that if not stopped, will soon make the world uninhabitable.

And that is where Russell and Mariko come in.

Russell captures an alien resistance fighter who explains that the two superpowers—The Republican Order and The Great Confederacy—have been assailing worlds like this for millennia. The reason is to squash any possible threat to their grip on galactic power while settling their disputes at the expense of the indigenous populations. Humanity is just such a threat. The only way to defeat both superpowers is to get them embroiled in an all-out war, off the planet—something they try to avoid at all costs.

Finally the alien tells Russell that there is a woman out there who has the genetic ability to access the portal to one of the alien ships—though she does not know this herself.

Instead of killing him, Russell believes the alien, and together they set out to find Mariko.

Meanwhile, Mariko is in the fight of her life, cornered by a horde of alien and human forces. All hope seems lost until Russell shows up with his crew and lays waste to the marauders.

Russell convinces Mariko of her destiny, and together they set out to find this portal. Along the way, they are relentlessly pursued and attacked by both superpower task forces, including a ruthless human collaborator playing both sides against the middle, DIRK POWERS. Regardless, they find the portal in Beijing's Forbidden City and teleport onto a Confederate ship.

While aboard, they meet up with other alien resistance fighters and Mariko's sister, YUKIKO. They take the ship and maneuver it out of orbit on a direct course to the Republican fleet.

Unbeknownst to the rebels, Powers sneaks aboard the ship and starts killing humans and aliens alike, attempting to sabotage the ship. Russell realizes this and takes on Powers in a mano-a-mano fight to the death, one that leaves Powers mortally wounded.

Powers dies, and Russell undoes the sabotage also dying in the process—martyred for his cause.

Pursued by other Confederate ships and facing a wall of destruction should they make it to the enemy armada, Mariko and the rest of the freedom fighters are resigned to their fates.

The Republican ships open fire upon the renegade Confederate ship. In battle, some of the Republican fire flies past the freedom fighters and hits the pursuing ships. The Confederate ships are programmed to return fire and do so, before their crews have a chance to override that directive. And lo and behold, ALL ships begin an epic space battle with the Earth as their backdrop.

Just before the renegade Confederate ship is destroyed, Mariko reopens the teleporter and pushes her unwilling sister through. Yukiko survives while Mariko and the alien resistance fighters are killed—becoming martyrs as well.

Soon thereafter, both Republican and Confederate forces are recalled from Earth. Nary a word is ever heard from either superpower again as the remnants of humanity begin to pick up the pieces of their broken world, whispering "Remember Russell and Mariko..." upon their lips.

Just as the logline implies, we have a sweeping story about average people doing extraordinary things under extreme circumstances. Can you imagine what it would be like if two alien superpowers had their proxy war on Earth? Just ask the people of North and South Vietnam. The logline is an allegory for a story that has played itself out time and again in human history.

The important thing to remember here is that the logline points you in the right direction. Keep it short and include only one or two people in the story. Also, real loglines come from what Blake Snyder used to call the *fun* part of the story (same for trailers). There'll be more on this later when we get into the *Three Cs of Story Structure,* but for now, just file this nugget away.

The logline combined with an ass-kicking title is a one-two punch that can really knock out a producer. When you hear them say, "Great, tell me more," you've got something going on.

Titles: Kicking Ass in as Few Words as Possible

JAWS, STAR WARS, THE GODFATHER, WHEN HARRY MET SALLY, CASABLANCA, DAWN OF THE DEAD, UNFORGIVEN, PULP FICTION, BLADE RUNNER, SILENCE OF THE LAMBS, GRINDHOUSE, SPARTACUS, GUESS WHO'S COMING TO DINNER, PRETTY WOMAN, CITIZEN KANE, AVATAR, THE PASSION OF THE CHRIST

What do all of these titles have in common?

They kick-ass. Even if you haven't seen some of these films, you know about them. They are as ingrained in American culture (and abroad) as football and McDonald's.

The titles for these movies say it all in as few words as possible. And that's the goal for you as a screenwriter.

If you pick an ambiguous title that doesn't create that "psychic itch" in the mind of the reader, they may not remember your story despite how good it is.

It's sad but true; you have to be a marketer long before you even get the chance to really market your scripts.

So how do you create a kick-ass title that complements your logline?

First ask yourself, can you sum up the story in one to five words? If you have a story about a 1940s milkman who sleeps with all of the lonely housewives and girlfriends of soldiers fighting overseas, you might want to call it something like: *Delivering Comfort*. Of course you don't want it to sound like a porno title, which are mostly farcical. So how about something a bit more era-centric, like *Stateside*?

The title implies that there are people (most likely military personnel) overseas and that there are loved-ones left home, i.e. stateside.

Now you give it a logline that delves deeper into the title and you end up with something like this:

STATESIDE

A romantic wartime drama with comedic elements

A draft-dodging milk deliveryman finds a fertile hunting ground of intimate liaisons with the lonely wives and girlfriends of soldiers fighting overseas during World War II. That is until the war ends.

With a logline and title combo like that, you can almost glean the entire synopsis of such a story.

- Draft dodger gets laid *all* the time from these lonely women.

- Draft dodger ultimately falls in love with soldier's wife who is not in love with her husband.

- The war ends and soldiers come home including wife's husband.

- A huge physical confrontation and emotional love triangle ensues over woman, complicated by the fact that she is married.

- Further complications arise as the protagonist's draft-dodging status is revealed and he is arrested and tried.

- Angry wife abandons draft dodger and chooses her husband and reconciliation.

- Draft dodger is sentenced and imprisoned but escapes.

- Draft dodger convinces wife to forgive him and run away with him.

- They end up living together in a South American country (with no extradition treaty with the U.S.) alongside NAZI war criminal expatriates.

The end of this story has an ironic twist against the *Stateside* title as the lovers are no longer living "stateside" but instead among the very enemies that their homeland went to war against.

So as you think about titles, remember to keep in mind that you are looking not only for a title to your work but a title that will complement your logline.

Witty or creative titles like *The Englishman Who Went Up a Hill but Came Down a Mountain* or *The Fast and the Furious* are all well and good but, if they leave the potential reader scratching their head, then you had better rethink your ingenuity. Also, try to avoid clichés with your titles. Calling a screenplay *All that Glitters* or *To Err Is Human* not only sounds corny but may be insulting to the reader. "Who is this guy to tell me that to err is human?!" Use something instead like *Rush Gold* or *Not at All Perfect!*

In the previous section, *Weakend Advances* and *Little War* adhere to this concept of story titles complementing loglines.

In *Weakend Advances*, Sarah does *advance* (or evolve) during her weekend's adventures. I could have titled it *Three Days in the Hamptons, Growing Up Sarah,* or *Love Is a Dish Best Served Cold,* but I want to keep it simple, catchy, and slightly ironic. Spelling *weekend* as "weakend" is a play on words, as being *weak* (which Sarah is at the beginning) and ostensibly the *end* for her love life, changes or *advances* to something else and something better by the end.

And as for *Little War,* the title suggests anything but. No war is little, certainly not one of interstellar proportions. And how are mere humans going to stop such omnipotent invaders? That's the irony. The title also is a double entendre as the so-called "little war" also means the proxy war on Earth for the alien superpowers, like Vietnam was for America and The Soviet Union.

The idea is to convey something original about your title and, by extension, your story as well.

Now you can look forward and see your story through to the end. Without that, where would you begin? You'd be floundering around trying to make a story fit your idea. However, with the basics out of the way—genre, loglines, and titles (that I presume you *will* write out before going on)—you're ready to jump right in and start creating actual characters.

Chapter Four: It's a Matter of Character

What Is a Great Character?

How are we doing so far? Have you started writing? If not, then you know what to do. I won't yell at you too much—right now. I'll just wait here patiently.

Okay, so here you are. You've started writing your story down. You've figured out the genre or genre hybrid. You've put together a working powerhouse logline that you'll refine as your story develops. And you've got a kick-ass title that makes me want to know more. The most important thing here is that you're writing, and you can see this story through to the end.

So now let's put some characters into your story. And by characters, I mean more than just the one or two people you've already written about in your logline.

What is a great character anyway? Is it some dude in the story that does the *protagonist* thing or the *antagonist* thing? Or is there a higher purpose for the characters? In other words, do you have main character X go from point A to point B and so on, hooking up with character Y and getting wrapped up in all kinds of intrigue? Sure, but that's not the only reason why you have character X and character Y.

If you were writing a set of stage instructions, a shot list, or even a shooting script, then maybe you'd make the character "do this and do that." But you're beyond that at this stage. If you don't write characters that take the reader on a serious journey (even in a comedy), that readers are going to care about, and that serve a true purpose to your story; you've got nothing.

Sure, add in "crazy uncle Eddie" or "slutty Nora Jean" or "bratty Danny-boy" and see where these caricatures and stereotypes of characters will get you. Nowhere.

Cliché characters are the most pedantic and frustrating elements of a movie that you are forced to sit through. Take for example a bad Sandra Bullock character (which there aren't too many of thankfully). In *The Proposal*, the female protagonist all out sucks!

Sorry Sandra, but it's true. She's been great in other movies like *Miss Congeniality*, *The Blind Side* (which earned her an Academy Award for Best Actress), and even in *Speed*. Why then does her performance in *The Proposal* fall flat?

One word: *stereotype*. How often do we see stories of career-driven women who lack the warmth and empathy to open themselves up to love until someone comes along that up-ends their world? Too many.

Not that that is a bad foundation for a character, but she never goes beyond that. She is a cliché of a cold fish who needs a man to warm her up. Boring!

Now take Julia Roberts as Vivian in *Pretty Woman*. She's a prostitute and makes no bones about it. She does everything to not let herself get emotionally involved with Richard Gere's character (Edward). However, as we learn more and more about her background, we can see her all business-like veneer start to dissolve. Her transformation is handled in a subtle, sub textual, and symbolic way (more on that later when we discuss *The Three Ss of Action and Dialogue*) very sublimely. Here's an example:

Vivian and Edward are at the opera together. Coincidentally enough, the opera being performed is Verdi's *La Traviata* or "The Woman Who Strayed," or "The Fallen Woman," or "The Tramp"—you get the idea. During the aria "Amami, Alfredo," Vivian is brought to tears. Why? Because that is an extremely powerful aria, a timeless story, and oh so symbolic. The same pain and delight (mentioned in Chapter One, but in this case, the anguish of love) that drives Verdi's Violetta to leave Alfredo for a greater good despite her love for him, affects Vivian and her burgeoning love for Edward.

Where's that same character arch for Sandra Bullock's forgettable character in *The Proposal*? *The Proposal* came out last year (2009) and no one remembers it. *Pretty Woman* came out twenty years ago and everyone remembers it!

The characters have a lot to do with that.

So how do we create memorable characters and avoid stereotypes? We utilize character *archetypes* as a foundation. I said *archetype* not *stereotype*—there's a big difference.

An archetype is an original symbol or motif of a person or thing.

A stereotype is an oversimplified image of a person or thing.

One is original; the other is a cheap copy.

Once you get the concept of original character archetypes down, you'll be able to delve deeper into developing and polishing these characters using *The Three Ps of Character Development*— more on that later.

Character Archetypes

What are we talking about here with character archetypes? Let's look at the difference between a particular character archetype and a character stereotype.

We used Julia Roberts' Vivian versus Sandra Bullock's Margaret previously, so we'll keep on this for a bit.

Vivian - Archetype	Margaret - Stereotype
A fallen woman - biblical like Mary Magdalene or operatic like Violetta A desire for love buried inside a broken spirit A dichotomy of characterization "sinner" (prostitute) and "angel" (inspires Edward to change from profiteer to benefactor)	A cold-hearted career-driven woman (as if career-driven women can't be warm and loving) Claims to have lost parents at young age and that's why she's cold, but that seems forced and too convenient to fit the story. If her life were a complete shambles because of the loss, then I'd buy it. Does nothing to help make Andrew (Ryan Reynolds) a better man who was defying his father anyway and pursuing his dream.

Vivian is clearly a great character archetype since she is so well remembered decades after we saw her on the silver screen.

Margaret, well... not.

Building upon the character archetype for Vivian, J.F. Lawton went deeper into developing all of her personal characterizations or character qualities that made her unique and allowed Julia Roberts to play her so well.

On the following page is another matchup of archetype vs. stereotype; this time we'll compare bad guys.

In one corner we have Roy Batty, the enigmatic ruthless yet sensitive Nexus 6 replicant from *Blade Runner*, in search of the meaning to his own existence, while also seeking to extend his meager four-year lifespan. In the other corner, we have the much talked about but rarely seen Lord Voldemort, evil wizard extraordinaire, from the *Harry Potter* films (based on the books). And for all of those Harry Potter fans who will certainly balk at whom I serve up as the stereotype bad guy, remember I'm only comparing the film versions of these characters.

Roy Batty - *Blade Runner*	Lord Voldemort - *Harry Potter*
Archetype - The Prodigal Son & Lost Soul	Stereotype - Vengeful Wizard
Born to be a slave with a four-year life span. Has an amazing crew of associates full of character and depth. When each one dies, you feel for them. We feel for Zhora when Deckard guns her down in cold blood. Pris has an air of innocence about her and truly loves Batty. Her death is gut wrenching. Leon laments for a childhood he never had, even keeping photographs of other people's lives as a means to placate his longings. "Nothing is worse than an itch you can't scratch," he tells Deckard. Returns to Earth to seek out his creator and reason for being. Kills only when he has to in order to survive. Kills Tyrell by thumbing in his eyes à la Oedipus Rex. Spares Deckard's life at the end (despite Deckard killing his entire crew) to make a point about how precious and fleeting life is.	He comes back from the dead but can't even beat Dumbledore in a fair fight, wizard-a-wizard. Has no real motivation (at least none that I've seen in the movies) to seek out revenge on Potter other than he's pissed. Boo, hoo. He killed Harry's parents (I'll give him that) but we never see him directly fuck with Harry enough to really establish Voldemort as anything other than a stereotypical bad guy. In other words, he provides *no* real opposition to Harry whatsoever. Has the worst crew of henchmen surrounding him that do not complement him in any way. Even Helena Bonham Carter as the raving Bellatrix Lestrange is painfully boring to watch. For three movies the hype built up over him never lives up to expectations when he finally shows up in *Harry Potter: The Goblet Of Fire*.

The winner of this bout: Roy Batty! Why? Because Batty's character is full of... well, character. He embodies The Three Ps (coming up in the next section), and connects immediately with the audience. Ridley Scott (director) and David Peoples (screenwriter) did an amazing job creating a so-called bad guy that you actually care about and end up rooting for in the end. And it helps that Rutger Hauer did a phenomenal job playing him—which catapulted his career into stardom back in the eighties.

Lord Voldemort, on the other hand, hardly earns the title "The Dark Lord." Come on. There's only one Dark Lord and that is Sauron from *The Lord of the Rings*. Sauron would only have to sneeze and Lord Voldemort would be vaporized instantly— that's even without the Ring of Power! Voldemort is a huge disappointment because he doesn't live up to the hype and has none of the *Ps* that would make him a great antagonist.

I'm sure I'm pissing off a lot of loyal Harry Potter fans here, and to be fair, the character was written for a series of children's novels. However, as Harry, Ron, and Hermione grow up and deal with adult issues like love, betrayal, sex, and death, so must the bad guys. Either the antagonists are real people (albeit wizards but people nonetheless) with real human qualities or they are simply caricatures and clichés. I guess we'll see how they are handled in the last two Harry Potter films coming up.

Here are some more character archetypes that we can look at without sinking down into stereotype hell.

- The Hero
- The Everyman
- The Forlorn or Heartbroken
- The Unrequited Lover
- The Lost Soul
- The Evil Bastard
- The Joker (no, not from Batman)
- The Whore (not limited to just prostitutes)
- The Bastard (different from The Evil Bastard)
- The Masochist
- The Sadist

- The Sado/Masochist
- The Despot
- The Sociopath
- The Angel
- The Muse
- The Heart of Gold
- The Prodigal Son
- The Femme Fatal
- The Treasure Seeker (obsessed & avaricious)
- The Dark Knight (no, not Batman himself)
- The Justice Seeker (justness or vengeance)

And so on. This list is by no means complete or definitive; it is just a sampling of the many archetypes that are available for the screenwriter to work with. Also, like genres, you can mix and match archetypes to come up with hybrid archetypes such as:

- The Heroic Bastard
- The Whore with a Heart of Gold
- The Evil Muse (inspires people to do bad things)
- The Sociopathic Lost Soul (not necessarily a killer)
- The Heartbroken Everyman
- The Angelic Unrequited Lover (always a bridesmaid never a bride)
- The Despotic Treasure Seeker
- The Dark Knight Justice Seeker (vengeful)

And so on.

Like with genre, your job is to discern the difference between a character archetype and a character stereotype. You can do this easily by watching movies with memorable characters, for example:

The Heroic Bastard - a.k.a. Han Solo

Who can forget this character? Here you have a man who is all about getting paid to save his own ass from the galactic mob boss (Jabba the Hutt) and will do anything for the huge reward.

He doesn't care about the rebellion or the empire or just about anything else but himself.

That's why HE SHOOTS FIRST in the cantina in *Star Wars*— because he's a bastard!

However, he's a hero. So how does that happen? Through the course of the first two decent *Star Wars* films, he learns about friendship, honor, fighting for a cause, and finally love. That's why his transformation is even greater than Luke's. Yeah he's a bastard, but a goddamn heroic one that all the ladies love— especially one particular headstrong princess.

The Angelic Sociopath - a.k.a. Catherine Tramell

Now here's a woman men love, up to a certain point—the point of an ice pick that is. In *Basic Instinct* she's seductive, alluring, exciting, cagey, mysterious, dangerous, sexual, maddening, intoxicating, addictive, and fatal.

And for a certain San Francisco cop, Nick Curran, she's the ticket to his undoing.

You never know whether Catherine is on the level or really psycho. The very definition of a sociopath is lacking any sort of conscience paired with antisocial behavior. Catherine certainly demonstrates that during the interrogation scene as she goads Nick and pisses off the police with her total lack of respect for the law.

You couldn't write a better badass character than Catherine, but you'll certainly try. Sharon Stone's character has been cheaply copied many times because writers seem to forget the very foundation of her archetype.

If you're gonna write an evil woman, go back to the basics: lust, greed, hatred, violence. Don't caricature her by making her a raving lunatic (Sharon Stone's Ginger in *Casino*—oh Sharon, what the hell happened to you here?) or some ridiculous supernatural creature (Megan Fox's Jennifer in *Jennifer's Body*). Real life is crazy enough. And the news is full of Catherine Tramells to draw upon: Amy Fisher, Amy Bishop, Pamela Smart, Andrea Yates, and Louise Woodward to name a few.

If you're stuck while trying to create a good character archetype or hybrid archetype, try doing the exercise I did with Batty versus Voldemort. Only this time, pit your character against a well-known and memorable movie character icon and see how they rate against each other. For example:

- Femme Fatale - Elsa Bannister, *The Lady from Shanghai*

- Everyman Hero - Dr. Richard Kimball, *The Fugitive*

- The Justice Seeker - Sarah Tobias, *The Accused*

- Unrequited Lover and Muse - Cyrano, *Cyrano de Bergerac*

- The Dark Knight (yes, Batman this time) - Bruce Wayne, *The Dark Knight*

Once you have the character archetypes for your main protagonist and antagonist figured out, then you can start putting together your killer cadre of memorable characters.

Assembling a Cadre of Memorable Characters

Okay fellow writers, you've determined what archetypes or hybrid archetypes of characters you want to work with; now you have to assemble the cast.

So the question is how many?

Well, to start with you need a protagonist (usually the "good" guy or gal—though not always the case), the antagonist (the "bad" guy or gal but really the opposition to the protagonist— you always need opposition in order to make a good story), and you need some supporting characters. That's it!

Well, not quite.

You can have more than one of each in terms of good and bad guys. Like in a rom-com, if you're telling a story about "boy meets girl" more often than not, you'll have boy and girl protagonists. However, if you want to spice things up a bit, the antagonist or antagonists can be the ex-girlfriend/boyfriend of the guy and gal throwing roadblocks in the way of the new lovers' path. Or, the boy and girl themselves can be both protagonists and antagonists to each other—as love can often be.

I'll repeat this again and again: you need opposition in order to make a good story. Whatever that opposing force is to your main characters (which may even be one of the main characters), you have to have it. No story can exist without some kind of challenge, confrontation, nemesis, conflict, archrival, etcetera, making life a living hell for the good guys. Even if your story is about bad guys, then the good guys (e.g., the police) are the opposition. You could make the police out to be corrupt or misleading and the gangsters Robin Hood-like. You know who the reader will root for.

Or, the opposition is nature, as in any number of disaster movies that have come out in the past few decades. Opposition can be aliens and their human collaborators (bent on taking over the world), a wild man-eating bear as in David Mamet's *The Edge* (though Alec Baldwin also provided human opposition to Anthony Hopkins' protagonist), or can be the person against himself, such as Bob Fosse's character in *All That Jazz* or Sid Vicious' character in *Sid and Nancy*.

The point being that no matter who your main characters are, you have to put them in harm's way, either by another character, nature, or themselves, or you don't have a *writable* story. Period.

If we go back to the discussion of the rules of genre, then the rom-com has really easy rules to follow.

- Boy meets girl
- Boy loses girl
- Boy gets girl back

With those rules in mind, you can easily put together the rest of the cast. Here's an example:

Though not a true rom-com, *Swingers* is a great example of a solid cadre of supporting characters to back up the protagonist.

Mike (Jon Favreau) is the protagonist. His archetype is The Forlorn. He spends much of the movie "not getting over" his ex-girlfriend. His buddies, Trent (Vince Vaughn), Mike's cousin Rob (Ron Livingston), and Sue (Patrick Van Horn) all do a remarkable job of complementing Mike's angst. They hold a mirror up to Mike's problems and character flaws and give him the much-needed kick in the ass to get his shit together.

Rob says to Mike about his ex, "She's a great girl and I love her but fuck her." In other words, Mike get over her and get the hell on with your life. Mike needs Rob to tell him that—that's what friends are for.

And Trent, holy shit, does he push Mike to get out of his comfort zone or what? Trent is an asshole (The Bastard archetype), and is more or less an antagonist to Mike, but it is his quasi-opposition that keeps pushing Mike to make different choices and step up when the time comes.

And that time is when Mike meets Lorraine (Heather Graham) at The Dresden.

There's more to Mike's posse, but you get the idea.

Since we've discussed a bunch of guys, let's talk now about a bunch of gals.

Sex and the City's ladies are the ultimate female buddy group. They're all protagonists and the entire show (and subsequent movies) couldn't exist without their unique dynamic. One female friend of mine told me that these women are *superheroes* to her!

Carrie Bradshaw (Sarah Jessica Parker) is the chief protagonist. Her gal-pals Samantha Jones (Kim Cattrall), Charlotte York (Kristin Davis), and Miranda Hobbes (Cynthia Nixon) make up a quartet that are American cultural icons of metro-glitz and glamour.

Carrie's archetype is The Unrequited Lover and Muse (with a bit of Angel and Hero sprinkled in). Samantha is well… The Whore with a Heart of Gold. Charlotte is The Lost Soul and Miranda is The Masochist with some Hero in her as well. Sometimes they are supporting protagonists to each other, and sometimes they are friendly antagonists to each other. That is why they are a memorable cadre of characters.

These are by no means absolute definitions, and I'm sure many hardcore *Sex and the City* fans would certainly dispute them; however, character archetypes are starting points not ending points. The next chapter will dive into giving your characters dimensions that will allow them and the actors who portray them to resonate with energy and veracity on the page and on the screen.

The salient point here is that when you are crafting your story, stick to a core group of characters that create the necessary dynamic to support your genre and story idea.

How many?

Start with two: protagonist and antagonist.

Add one or two supporting characters for each.

And then stop!

Four you say! Only four characters?

Well, in the broadest sense, you'll find that you don't need much more than that. Of course, if the story demands it, then add more main characters; just make sure you flesh them out as richly as the first four.

In my Boston-based rom-com, *Opportunity Knockout*, I have Mike O'Connell (the male protagonist) and his best friend Brian Pandolini, Alison Angelina (the female protagonist) and her best friend Stacey Greene. These four make up the core of my story. From there I added several external characters that are in support and opposition to the leads. But generally, the story is about the four—more specifically Mike and Alison, whom I mentioned before in the rom-com genre can be both protagonists and antagonists to each other.

Four is all you need. Sure, you'll need other characters to come and go and play off your main characters, but don't go to great lengths to make them your main characters.

Take a look at *Die Hard*.

The story is about two characters: John McClane (Bruce Willis) and Hans Gruber (Alan Rickman). That's it!

Sure there's McClane's wife Holly; and McClane's cop buddy (via radio) Al; and Karl, the guy who wants McClane deader than dead, but they are all supporting characters. The real story here is a "cat and mouse" game between McClane and Gruber. Protagonist versus Antagonist. Everything else is eye-candy.

Look, if you're Peter Jackson, you can write the adaptation to Tolkien's *Lord of the Rings* and have the big ensemble cast. But since you're a newbie screenwriter, don't take on something that you're not ready to handle. You'll never get a sweeping epic even looked at by producers, et al., if you're still wet behind the ears in this game. Keep it small, keep it simple—master the craft.

And with that, we can begin coloring in your characters with the magic *Three Ps of Character Development*.

Oh, but first, put the goddamn book down and succinctly write up who your four main characters are going to be: protagonist and antagonist, their archetypes, and how they rate against famous ones of their ilk while avoiding cliché caricatures. Don't spend too much time on this; you've got way more important stuff to work on here.

When you're done, then turn to the next page.

Chapter Five: The Three Ps of Character Development

What Is Good Character Development?

In all good character development that I've ever seen, especially when it comes to screenwriting, there is one common element: The Three Ps.

- Past

- Problem

- Panache

The Three Ps of Character Development are important when crafting a character that the reader (and hopefully someday the viewing audience) will love and remember. If choosing the right archetype for your character is like the block of stone for your sculpture, then character development is the chiseling of that stone into a rough sculpture. The polishing of that sculpture will come in the form of action and dialogue (which is discussed in the next chapter).

If you have poor and forgettable characters in your story, no one is going to read past the first few pages. If you have mediocre and boring characters but a really great story, no one is going to buy your story, even if they read it. However, if your characters jump off the page and the story captures the reader's interest, then you are looking at a sellable story. More importantly, you are looking at a "writable" story.

If you can't believe in your characters then how will anyone else? You and your audience need to fall in love with these characters, need to love and hate these characters, and need to empathize with the characters. Movies only have a finite amount of time to get the audience to really care about the characters—even the evil ones.

Take Michael Corleone (Al Pacino) in *The Godfather*. Yes, he's a gangster, but he's also a war hero, an eventual father, a husband, and a loyal son. He does what he has to in order to save his family in the often-fatal world of the criminal underground. Mario Puzo created a character of diametrically opposed archetypes and further colored him with an elegant style of sensitivity, ruthlessness, and honor.

Michael embodies The Three Ps to a tee. His *past* involves being born into a mafia family, as well as being a war hero. His *problem* involves resolving his personal desires to live a life outside of the criminal world while also defending his family from rival families bent on killing the Corleones. And his *panache* is that he is *cool-headed* and makes very careful and calculated decisions, unlike his *hot-headed* brother Sonny (which gets him killed). Also, Michael is soft-spoken and tender towards his wife, Kay (Diane Keaton), yet merciless when dealing with the enemies of the Corleone family. Case in point, the scene in the restaurant where Michael dispassionately kills the men behind his father's assassination attempt.

This is how you create a memorable character and with memorable characters you can create a memorable story—the kind of story a person with the right clout will read and buy—and maybe, just maybe, get produced.

Let's look at each of the Ps more closely.

Past

All great characters have to have a serious past. In fact, all characters should have some kind of past. In screenwriting, however, there is little time to delve too deeply into anyone's past. Most of the time, you are usually playing *catch-up* learning about the character as you go. But there are many great ways in which to introduce a character's past that is totally relevant to the actions and decisions they make in the present—on film.

Take for example Tom Cruise's character, Nathan Algren, from *The Last Samurai*. Here's a real tortured soul with a lot of baggage. After having witnessed one too many massacres during the American Civil War, he takes his demons with him to Japan as a mercenary training Japanese conscripts into a professional standing army for the Japanese emperor. During this time, he is captured by the old bushido-following samurai after a fierce battle and nursed back to health. He eventually adopts the ways of the samurai and even helps Katsumoto's (Ken Watanabe) warriors make one last stand against the emperor's army and the encroaching Westernization of the Japanese culture.

The point of Algren is that he wouldn't have thrown-in with Katsumoto and his beliefs if Algren hadn't been through hell in war himself. There is an understanding between these men who have both seen too much blood and suffering. Cruise is able to abandon his mercenary position and strive for a nobler endeavor because of his past and the redemption he seeks—even if it may cost him his life.

Here's another example: In *Casablanca*, Ilsa Lund (Ingrid Bergman) has a past to reckon with as much as Rick Blaine (Humphrey Bogart). Her husband, Victor Laszlo (Paul Henreid) a resistance leader, is an enemy of the Nazi regime. During the time Ilsa and Rick spent in Paris together before the events in Casablanca, Morocco, Ilsa was married to Victor, who was locked away at a Nazi concentration camp. She presumed he was dead and decided to follow her heart and fall in love with Rick. Just before the Nazis invade Paris, the two lovers decide to go on the run together. However, Ilsa finds out that her husband is still alive and she abandons Rick for her marriage and a greater cause (helping her husband fight the Nazis).

When they meet a year later, Rick is royally pissed at Ilsa. What he doesn't realize is that Ilsa is plagued by demons of her past, forcing her to make some heart-wrenching decisions—especially when it comes to Rick. She's a mess and that shines through, making her character one of the most memorable in cinematic history.

So, your characters should have a past to contend with in some form or another. You need not spend too much time dwelling on your character's past, but with a few properly placed flashbacks or lines of dialogue, you can get the audience up to speed that this person has skeletons in their closet. This makes for a more interesting character and a better writing, and reading experience.

Problem

What good would a character be if they didn't have problems to deal with in the their daily lives? Even in *Confessions of a Shopaholic*, Rebecca Bloomwood (Isla Fisher) has her share of problems: compulsive shopping and mounting debt. These problems of hers drives her character to make both smart and not-so-smart decisions. For example: she takes a lesser job at a subsidiary magazine as a means to work her way up to a position in the parent magazine that she really wants (and pay off her debts)—smart. She lies to her boss (and love interest), hypocritically spends money, and racks up even more debt, even while she's writing about saving money—not-so-smart. She avoids the collection agent like the plague and paints him out to be a stalker ex-boyfriend—not-so-smart. Finally, she holds an auction to sell all of her frivolous stuff, ultimately paying off her debt—very smart.

Her problems seem like they will overwhelm her, isolate her from people who care about her (her boss/boyfriend and her best friend), and eventually ruin her financially. However, once she decides to take action and address her problems, Rebecca starts to change for the better and things eventually work out for her and her relationships.

The problem or problems a character faces is also known as the conflict or the opposition. They are not necessarily internal struggles but can be external, as in other people opposing the main character or protagonist's goals. Hence the *antagonist*.

Take for example the movie *Strange Days*. Ralph Fiennes as Lenny Nero is constantly facing opposition from whom he thinks is his best friend, Max Peltier (Tom Sizemore). In fact, for most of the movie as Lenny tries to uncover this so-called conspiracy in the LA police department that is responsible for some notable celebrity killings, his trail of clues are being laid out by Max, leading Lenny to his ultimate demise. All along, Lenny has his own problems as he struggles with an addiction to the new technology of replaying recordings of people's memories in his own head—especially his own memories of his ex-girlfriend Faith (Juliette Lewis).

The tension created is great as Lenny is surreptitiously *blocked at every turn* by Max. When the final betrayal is revealed (both Max and Faith colluding together as killers and lovers), Lenny almost collapses from grief, and the audience feels totally connected to Lenny at that pivotal moment. The showdown between Lenny and Max is classic *brother against brother* symbolism.

Bottom line, when creating your characters, think about what problems they might have both internally and externally that will drive their actions and the story forward. Creating conflict or opposition is the soul of great screenwriting.

Panache

What the hell is panache, you might ask. Panache is a flamboyant confidence or style of manner in one's character. Lots of great characters throughout history have had panache: Hamlet (after he goes mad), Cyrano de Bergerac, Lawrence of Arabia, Scarlett O'Hara, Mary Rose Foster (a send-up of Janis Joplin in the movie *The Rose*), Han Solo (from episodes IV and V of the *Star Wars* saga), and Miranda Priestly from *The Devil Wears Prada* to name a few.

Panache is that special something that sets your characters apart from the dull wooden figures you see in the worst movies—and believe me, they are unfortunately too numerous to mention. You couldn't care less what happens to those types of characters. And they are as forgettable as that disappointing fancy dinner you had last week in that posh restaurant.

Your characters can have either oodles of panache or be subtler about it. Your characters do not have to be James Bond in order to have style and charm and a sense about them that makes you want to care for them. For example, in *Avatar*, Jake Sully (Sam Worthington) is an everyman grunt, who finds himself in an extraordinary situation as he tries to save this native alien tribe from being destroyed by corporate mercenaries. Jake is not as flamboyant as James Bond; however, he does have a subtle sense of doing the right thing after he's seen what's really happening on the planet Pandora. He starts out as a grunt, but he learns, changes, and evolves due to his past (an injury that left him a paraplegic), his problems (loving a native woman and her tribe in the face of their destruction), and his acerbic panache, as he learns the ways of the Na'vi and becomes one of them.

You end up caring about Jake and his plight, even though he's more reserved than his co-star's character Grace Augustine, played by the forceful Sigourney Weaver. And of course, Stephen Lang's performance as Colonel Miles Quaritch is all-out badass (and full of The Three Ps).

Panache is not something that you can give your characters right off the bat. This quality has to grow on its own as you write and rewrite the characters in your story. And really, you'll only infuse the main characters and some supporting ones with great panache. Some will be good guys with hearts of gold despite adversity, some will be brazen SOBs who will walk over anyone in order to get to the top, some will be funny or irascible (or both), some will be BFFs through thick and thin, etcetera.

Don't think of panache as *over the top* theatrics because that's more caricature than character. Think of panache as that gem that makes your character stand out in some way, even for a few moments. Then the reader will be forever sold on them.

Ps Give Characters Personality

Let's take a quick look at examples of characters and their associated Ps on the following page. By doing the following simple exercise, you can see if your characters have enough *personality* to rate as memorable and interesting. For this exercise, I'm going to make up a few notable character archetypes and then throw some Ps on them and see if I can make a story here.

Character	Veteran Cop	Ambitious Actress	Budding Ponzi Schemer
Archetype	*Hero & Lost Soul*	*Muse & Dark Angel*	*Evil Bastard & Everyman*
Past	Got his partner killed (and covered it up) while investigating the murder of an actress with a past.	Grew up in a poor mid-west town. Ran away to make it big.	Grew up next to Ambitious Actress, in-love with her. Ran away to find her and make it big as well.
Problem	Case keeps rearing its ugly head, taunting the cop to solve. Blocked at every turn by powerful enemies.	Can't get legitimate acting jobs. Turns to adult films under pseudonym and disguise. Sleeps her way into mainstream movie roles but eventually is found out.	Responsible for killing Ambitious Actress out of jealousy. Veteran Cop getting closer to catching him. Maintains a charitable foundation while bilking people out of millions.
Panache	Drinks and gambles too much to forget his shame. Hot-headedness gets him suspended often.	Quotes moral platitudes from the bible while performing sex scenes. Her alter-ego is a free-spirit and an inspiration to others.	Talks like an evangelist preaching investment opportunities while destroying businesses and shipping jobs overseas.

As you can see above, not only have I created three very strong and tangible characters but, through the exercise, I have managed to weave them together into the makings of a story.

LAMBS AND LIONS

A Crime Drama

A cop, an actress, and a businessman, all with something to hide, collide in the City of Angels where only the devils live.

Now go and write up The Three Ps for each of your main characters. Don't spend too much time on this exercise. Don't write more than a page on each character. And don't worry yourself into a tizzy if you can't get all the Ps right off. Like people, characters take time to learn and grow. Getting your character to go from a simple Everyman to an Anti-Hero with a substance-abuse problem because he failed at saving someone's life and now has to deal with the deceased person's sister with whom he has fallen hopelessly in love while using his rapier wit and musical talents to woo, takes a while to get.

The *Three Ps of Character Development* give your characters that memorable P: *personality*.

Are you ready to start beating out your story? If so, then here we go with *The Three Cs of Story Structure*.

Chapter Six: The Three Cs of Story Structure

If You Build it, They Will Come

Many books have been written about screenplay structure. Everyone has a take on how a writer should lay out their script. For example:

Robert Mckee (*Story: Substance, Structure, Style and The Principles of Screenwriting*) uses terms like *inciting incident, arc-plot, controlling idea,* and *story climax.*

David Trottier (*The Screenwriter's Bible*) and Syd Field (*Screenplay: The Foundations of Screenwriting*) are all about *catalyst, crisis, pinch point, final showdown,* etcetera.

And Blake Synder (*Save the Cat! The Last Book on Screenwriting You'll Ever Need*) liked to use his *beat sheet* or the BS2 (**B**lake **S**nyder **B**eat **S**heet) to structure screenplays. There's even a BS2 app for the iPhone®!

All of these methods are fine means to an end. However, I'm not a huge fan of organized story structure dictating that your story has to have *this* happen by *this* page. As I have learned over the years, no one style of story structure fits every story. In fact, there are so many story concepts, genres, film styles, running times, and types of productions (films, TV episodes, mini-series, documentaries, news reports, and so-called reality shows) that a writer must employ different and varied story structures that adapt to whatever their material requires.

However, at a 20,000-foot-level view, there are always common elements in a screenplay for a dramatic, comedic, or reality-based presentation. Those are The Three Cs of Story Structure. The Three Cs are: the Catalyst, the Crisis, and the Corollary (or Conclusion—sometimes Climax, but that implies nothing important happens afterwards). Or, to be more time-honored and classical about it, *The Aristotelian Model of Story-Telling.* Aristotelian as in Aristotle, the Ancient Greek philosopher, whose theory of poetics included the idea of a whole story having a beginning, middle, and end. There's more to it than that, but suffice it to say that the implication here is a traditional three-act structure serving as the best vehicle to tell your story. And it seems to work well.

If you break down a script into acts as they are generally written, you will note that each of the Cs corresponds to an act in a three-act screenplay. This is the general structure for most films. However there are exceptions: a one-hour drama on television will have four to five acts (possibly including a teaser and an epilogue), a movie-of-the-week can have seven, and a mini-series might have twelve.

But since we're talking about screenwriting feature films here, we'll stick with three acts.

So what happens and when, you might ask. Let's look at each act and its corresponding C from our 20,000 feet up in the air.

Act One: Catalyst

Here's a simple plot for a drama that should illustrate the concept of the *catalyst*.

- FBI Agent collars the big Mob Boss.
- Mob Boss' henchmen kill FBI Agent's family.
- FBI Agent grieves and then vows revenge.
- Mob Boss walks due to rigged trial, flees country.
- FBI Agent hunts Mob Boss down and now must face an entire army of henchmen alone.
- End of Act One.

So where's the catalyst in this first act? Obviously, it must be when the FBI Agent's family was killed. Or was it when the FBI Agent caught the Mob Boss? Or was it when the Mob Boss walks and flees the country? Or how about when the FBI Agent hunts down the Mob Boss and now must take on dozens of hired guns by himself?

The answer is all of the above. The entire first act is, in my opinion, the catalyst. Sure, there are major plot points and turning points, but by the end of the first act, the entire stage is set for a huge battle of guns, wits, souls, grit, and guts. For example: how is the FBI Agent going to take on all of these guys? Will the Mob Boss get the upper hand and finish the job on the FBI Agent? Can the FBI Agent bring the Mob Boss to justice or will he kill him outright? Who's going to help the FBI Agent? Does the FBI Agent go rogue in order to take down the Mob

Boss? Does the Mob Boss have a weakness that the FBI Agent can exploit?

There are literally dozens of ways the writer can go with this. But it all comes down to the catalyst in Act One. I suggest working out the end of Act One first before you start writing from the beginning. Once you know how Act One is going to end and where everyone is going to be, then you can backtrack and fire off the whole act, feeling confident you'll carry the story swimmingly for the next 25 to 30 pages.

Let's take a quick look at *Chinatown*'s Act One.

- Private detective Jake Gittes (Jack Nicholson) is hired by Mrs. Evelyn Mulray (wife of LA's water commissioner, Hollis Mulray) to find out if he's seeing another woman.

- Jake tails Hollis Mulray across LA through different areas that have to do with LA's water distribution system.

- The real antagonist, Noah Cross, is subtly introduced via a photograph taken during the investigation of Cross and Mulray arguing.

- Jake eventually catches Mr. Mulray with another woman and photographs them together.

- The photos end up in the newspaper. Jake takes some flack for it.

- The *real* Mrs. Evelyn Mulray (Faye Dunaway) shows up with her lawyer and slaps a lawsuit on Jake.

- Jake investigates who set up both him and Hollis Mulray, finding clues along the way that will be big payoffs later on in Act Three.

- Jake goes to see Hollis Mulray at his home but encounters Evelyn. She drops the lawsuit and wants to forget the whole thing. He won't let it go. Evelyn tells Jake where he might find Hollis.

- At a reservoir, the police have cordoned off the area as Jake shows up. Jake has a few words with his old police colleague, Lt. Escobar, and learns that Hollis Mulray has been killed. Mulray's body is dragged from the reservoir missing a shoe and his glasses (more setups for later). The game is on, and that's a perfect break into Act Two.

There are literally dozens of setups throughout the first act that I haven't even touched upon. The level of subtlety, subtext, and symbolism (discussed later in Chapter Seven) is astounding, and the examples are too numerous to mention. Suffice it to say, Roman Polanski (director) and Robert Towne (screenwriter) crafted a seminal masterpiece of both cinematic and screenwriting perfection. And it wasn't easy. The original draft came in at about 180 pages. There were lots of arguments and rewrites to get the page count down and to produce a two-hour-and-ten-minute work of art that still holds up today.

In fact, a movie like this probably couldn't get made today, due to the intensity of its story and a very down ending. But that doesn't mean you shouldn't try to write something like *Chinatown*. Write the best story you can and worry about selling it later.

And so without a good Act One, you'll never figure out how you're going to break into Act Two and continue on. That's where all the *fun* is in the movie as Blake Snyder used to say.

Act Two: Crisis

Here's where all the action heats up. Act Two is the roller coaster ride of action, hijinks, journey of introspection, and the overall *fun* part of the movie for the 60 pages or so. In fact, most of the movie trailers you see take the majority of scenes from the Act Twos of their films. This is also true for the loglines used to sell story concepts to producers.

Take for example *The Dark Knight*.

If you watch the trailer closely, you see Batman (Christian Bale) riding the Bat Pod facing down The Joker (Heath Ledger) on the streets of Gotham, the funeral for Police Commissioner Loeb (the scene where James Gordon gets ostensibly killed), and the crashing of the Bruce Wayne party by The Joker. All of these scenes and more were taken from Act Two of the film.

But if you look at what those scenes represent, they clearly spell out the crisis of the movie: STOP THE JOKER!

The Joker has his own agenda as well: KILL THE BATMAN! And also terrorize Gotham.

Furthermore, during the crisis stage of the story, there is: the death of Rachel Dawes, the disfigurement of Harvey Dent and the rise of his ruthless alter ego Two-Face, the death of a lot of people, and Bruce Wayne's grief over losing the woman he loves.

All of this is a great setup for the final corollary or confrontation/climax of Act Three.

But before we can get to Act Three, let's delve a bit deeper into what makes a good movie crisis and setup for the big finale.

A good Act Two crisis should have the following qualities:

- The main character(s) situation has changed from equilibrium to chaos.

- The main opposition is fully in play here. Again, you need *opposition* or *conflict* in order to have a real story to tell.

- There are reveals and more questions at every turn.

- There is a rise to the challenge or a fall from grace, or both.

- When love is involved, the lovers get together and then split up.

- Some of the best action is showcased here.

- Setups from Act One DO NOT get paid off here; only more setups are peppered into Act Two. These payoffs will happen in Act Three.

And there you have it—the breadth of Act Two for 55 to 65 pages of excitement. By the mid-point, you'll see that everything in the main character's world will be totally out of whack. That is the point of no return. You should always keep the reader guessing as to what is going to happen next. Here's a romantic comedy example of an Act Two layout:

THE LONELY HEARTS PUB

A Romantic Romp with Reality-style Sequences

Two star-crossed lovers meet in a place where only the lonely are allowed to play: reality TV.

In Act One, KYLE ROSS and MICHELLE PARKER, who appear on separate reality shows, are both publicly dumped by their respective SOs. Along with their humiliation and the pain of their losses, there seems to be a run of bad luck. Kyle loses his apartment and has to move back in with his mother, and Michelle finds out that she's being sued by her ex for a collection of

Hummels they picked up in Europe. Both Kyle and Michelle vow to never get involved again. Instead, they go drinking with their friends and all accidentally end up at a place called (you guessed it!) *The Lonely Hearts Pub*. Michelle spills a drink on Kyle [the *cute meet* in rom-com terminology]. The two hit if off, dance together, throw darts, get drunker, talk about how much relationships suck, and sleep together. The next day is awkward, and both decide to wish each other well, not intending to ever see each other again.

Here's what happens to them in Act Two:

MR. SLICK TV producer (and so-called friend to Kyle) cons him to go on another reality show.

Michelle is offered the same deal by Mr. Slick with the added incentive of getting the lawsuit dropped.

Unbeknownst to each other, Kyle and Michelle end up on the same reality show, which forces them to spend an awful lot of time together. Over the course of the show, they start to develop true feelings for each other

Mr. Slick is betting that the ratings from all of this tension between two jilted lovers will be a boon for him and his career. Furthermore, to spice things up, he constantly tries to put up roadblocks to keep Kyle and Michelle from connecting with the help of other studs and babes coming on to the show.

Despite the challenges, Kyle and Michelle do fall in love. They vow to leave the show together.

Mr. Slick can't allow that, so he brings their exes on to the show (Kyle's ex is also a producer at the same network as Mr. Slick), and through a series of contrived encounters with the exes, he succeeds in breaking up Kyle and Michelle.

Mr. Slick quietly pays off Michelle's ex to drop the lawsuit and propose to her, agreeing to have the wedding ceremony aired on national TV.

Act Two ends with a huge blowout on the show between Kyle and Michelle. Kyle leaves the show. The ratings go through the roof as Michelle (who's pissed off at Kyle) forgives her ex and accepts his proposal! Mr. Slick is on top of the world, and the two star-crossed lovers are in the depths of despair.

How is all of this going to get resolved?

Don't ask me! You're the writer. You've established all the tension and opposition necessary along with carefully placed setups that can now be paid off in Act Three. The goal here is that for the last act, you have to get them back together and bring down Mr. Slick—and you have to do it on the show for the proverbial icing on the cake!

Now it is time to *break that third act!*

Act Three: Corollary

Coming to the conclusion of a screenplay's story line seems simple enough, right? Wrong. It is anything but. Act Three, the third and final act has to pay off for the audience in some significant way or the entire effort has been for naught. Don't get me wrong. In *Kill Bill: Volume Two* (KB2), there is a seemingly huge let down at the end with a lot of talk and barely any action—especially between Beatrix (Uma Thurman) and Bill the late David Carradine. Here the audience is expecting a real sword-wielding showdown, and instead you get a bunch of witty banter and a brief flash of action before Beatrix quickly dispatches Bill with the Five Point Palm Exploding Heart Technique.

What a disappointment! Well, not really. You see, Quentin Tarantino had been setting up an emotional and philosophical confrontation between Beatrix and Bill ever since *Volume One*. Here's what I mean:

Taken separately, one can argue that there simply is no real act structure to KB2 and the third act definitely falls apart with some somber melodramatic dialogue and little action. However, when you look at KB1 and KB2 as *one* movie, then you see the overall structure and the setups for the cathartic climax at the end. All throughout the combined movie, Tarantino has been laying down the groundwork for both Beatrix and Bill's motivations for their actions. Beatrix wants both revenge and eventually her daughter back. Her whole reason for going off the reservation from Bill was because she was pregnant and wanted a better life for her baby than that of an assassin. Bill wanted revenge after being jilted by Beatrix, but is now remorseful over what he had done to her. This is why he tells Elle Driver (Daryl Hannah) not to kill Beatrix when she's lying in a coma. Also, I believe that when it came down to the final fight between Bill and Beatrix he basically let her beat him—his heart just wasn't into it anymore. Sure, maybe she could have taken him in a fair fight, but I think in homage to *Star Wars*, Tarantino did an Obi Wan Kenobi with Bill. Obi Wan sacrificed himself for Luke Skywalker's survival and benefit. Bill does the same here for his daughter's sake. With his whole team of assassins wiped out by Beatrix, and the epiphany that she might be right, I think Bill was ready to let her take B.B. (the daughter) and call it a day.

You wouldn't get all of that pay-off from Tarantino if you had a straight action ending. Tarantino was giving you a genre sampling all the way through both movies, while laying down subtext about greater issues such as family, loyalty, justice, and changes of heart.

That's corollary. In fact the very definition of corollary is "a direct or natural consequence or result." After all that revenge-getting, what else would satisfy the conclusion of that story? Bill dies rather anti-climatically but with pride, and Beatrix gets her daughter back.

Granted, *Kill Bill* is a more complicated representation of the Act Three Corollary (that's the genius of Tarantino), so let's go back to our star-crossed lovers Kyle and Michelle and see if we can't find a corollary other than simply getting them back together.

When last we left our pair of unfortunate paramours, they were broken up, and Mr. Slick was at the top of his game. So what next?

Kyle finds out that they were betrayed or setup by Mr. Slick (his supposed friend) from the beginning.

Kyle learns of the pending wedding while drinking at the Lonely Hearts Pub. Kyle left the show, but now realizes that he must get back on at all costs to talk to Michelle and win her back. He decides to act and enlists the help of his producer ex-girlfriend—who's had a change of heart about Kyle and Michelle's true love.

Michelle's not stupid and knows something is up. She decides to play along, having agreed to marry her ex live on national television. She manages to sneak into the editing van of the film crew and sees a video of her fiancé on the phone with Mr. Slick. She takes out an MP3 player and records the audio.

Meanwhile, with the help of his buddies and his ex, Kyle storms on to the set and crashes the wedding while being chased by security, all live on TV. Kyle's ex keeps the show from getting pulled off the air during all of this chaos. This actually causes the ratings to soar.

Just before the vows are made, Kyle confronts Michelle with the truth. She rebuffs him; Kyle is dejected.

The wedding continues and the vows are made but instead of saying, "I do," Michelle says, "I do not!" She tells the viewing audience that she discovered that she and Kyle had been set up by Mr. Slick and produces from her corset her MP3 player and plays the recording between her now ex-fiancé and Mr. Slick.

The camera pans over to Mr. Slick who is mortified—the reality show "reality bubble" has been burst. Slick's phone rings; his boss demands his presence. The fiancé shrinks back. Kyle is elated. Michelle runs into his arms, and the two take off like Dustin Hoffman and Ali McGraw in *The Graduate*. The final shot is of them dancing the night away together (Michelle still in her wedding dress) at the Lonely Hearts Pub with all of their friends celebrating with them.

You see it is not enough to simply get them back together. You have to have payoff and resolution to the outstanding issues in order to satisfy the audience and write a compelling story. When you create opposition, that opposition must get its comeuppance. Or, if the theme of the story is that "evil will prevail," then the opposition are the "good guys" who fail to stop the "bad guys" but give it a hell of a try.

You have to pepper that second act with setups that will help your characters along to the finish line in Act Three. Even while writing this, I went back to the Act Two synopsis and added necessary setups to help my Act Three work.

Here is an example of an act breakdown for my rom-com, *Opportunity Knockout*:

Act One:

- At the height of the dot-com bubble, companies and individuals throw around money like it was confetti. Rampant greed and materialism affects the whole country like a plague. It seems like the good times will never end.

- MIKE O'CONNELL and ALISON ANGELINA are introduced. He works for ProTek (a ruthless executive staffing firm), and she works for Athenaeum (an ethical yet struggling executive staffing firm).

- Athenaeum's president, JOE MCCASEY, and his son, JAMES MCCASEY, are like a father and brother to Alison, and are as ethical as they come. In fact, Alison goes to great length to be unlike her late father (Thomas Vincent Angelina, a former business partner and friend of Joe's), who ultimately died an unethical businessman.

- The biggest ad agency in Boston announces a multi-million dollar exclusive contract to one lucky staffing firm.

- Mike is entrusted by his nefarious boss, LARRY HURTZ, with a book of staffing scams (referred to as "The Book") to help his company win the contract.

- Mike and Alison separately get drunk while out on the town with friends (BRIAN PANDOLINI, Mike's friend; STACEY GREENE, Alison's friend). They tumble into each other (meeting for the first time) while trying to get the same taxi. Sparks fly between them. They make a date for the following week.

- In the process, Mike loses The Book. It falls into the cab and ultimately into Alison's possession by the end of the act.

Act Two:

- Mike is "shitting bricks" knowing that when his boss finds out, he'll ruin Mike's career. Brian tries to buck him up.

- Alison reluctantly uses The Book to start helping her firm win the contract. She falls ever more under the spell of this mysterious tome. She even uses it to get Stacey a job at the hottest ad agency in town that she's totally not qualified for.

- Mike reluctantly scams an executive, DOUG VALENTINI (an old friend of Alison's family), out of the running for a job at a youth-image dot-com due to his age.

- Mike and Alison start dating. They eventually fall in love with each other.

- Brian has a great scene with his dot-com company, declaring an unofficial office holiday where the whole staff takes off for a yacht ride, a lobster lunch by the sea, and cocktails at a prominent Boston strip club.

- Alison's company wins the contract.

- Hurtz finds out about the loss of The Book and orders Mike to steal it back. Mike is shocked to learn that his now girlfriend, Alison, has it.

- Mike gets the chance to steal it when he and Alison are about to make love for the first time at her place. Mike decides *not to steal it* because he loves her.

- Mike is fired and professionally ruined by his now ex-boss.

- Hurtz calls the Department of Justice on Alison and her company.

- Alison is fired from her company. Joe is devastated by her actions that now put the very future of the company in jeopardy.

- Alison returns The Book back to Hurtz. He tells her that Mike was sent to get it from her. Alison is shocked and enraged by this. What's worse is that the author of The Book turns out to be none other than Alison's deceased father. She freaks.

- While playing basketball, Mike tells Brian that he's going to confess everything to Alison and hopes she'll understand. Then they notice her driving up to the court like a crazy person.

- Alison beats the crap out of Mike and breaks up with him. Brian helps him get to a hospital.

- Stacey is found out at work that she can't do the job she was hired for. She's subsequently fired.

- The dot-com bubble bursts and the economy goes to hell. Brian also loses his job. The good times are over.

- Joe manages to save his company but almost dies of a heart attack in the process.

- Alison secretly visits him in the hospital and vows to set things right. End of Act Two.

Act Three:

- Alison is now working for Hurtz at ProTek. She searches for a way to bring the company down.

- While Mike is looking for "honest" work, Brian comes to say goodbye. He's motorcycling across country to California to hang with his surfer-dude grandpa. Afterwards, Mike decides to help an unemployed Doug get the job of his dreams. Mike promises the means will be legitimate. Doug reluctantly agrees to let Mike help him.

- Alison allies herself with LAURA, Hurtz's mistress and a cold-blooded recruiter in her own right. She is pissed that Hurtz gave Mike The Book and not her. Laura wants what she deserves and decides to give Alison "the goods" on Hurtz.

- Mike uses some theatrics to get Doug in front of the CEO of Boston's most prestigious investment firm. Doug then does the rest to wow the guy.

- Alison and Stacey sneak into ProTek after hours. Stacey uses her good looks to distract the security guard while Alison finds "the goods" that Laura told her about.

- At a huge shareholders meeting for ProTek held in The Four Seasons Hotel in Boston, Alison leads a legion of scammed executives (Doug is one of them) and the authorities into the massive ballroom to confront Hurtz. Alison shows the evidence, and Hurtz and his cronies are taken away. Doug subsequently tells Alison how Mike helped him.

- Alison is forgiven by her Joe and James and has rejoined her old company, now as VP of Operations.

- Mike runs into Stacey who tells him that Alison still loves him, and he has to fight for her if he wants her back.

- Mike is inspired to *storm the office* at Athenaeum to find Alison. Security chases him around.

- Mike finds Alison in a conference room giving a presentation. He bursts in. She is surprised to see him.

- Mike professes his love to her and goes on about how everything means nothing to him without her.

- Alison wants to believe him but asks him for references. Mike says he has none, but Alison tells him that Doug vouched for him. She forgives him.

- Alison kisses Mike and the entire staff cheers for them. The End.

Though the Act Three breakdown is more detailed, the amount of pages is only thirty-one and reads very fast—third acts typically run about 20 to 30 pages. The difference between this type of breakdown and a treatment/synopsis is that here I mark all of the setups and payoffs. Also, I briefly touch on the subplots of the story. The important thing here is to get a 20,000-foot view, mapping out the plot twists and turns, and making sure The Three Cs are applied appropriately.

This is a good exercise when revising your screenplay *after* you've written the first draft.

Later, in Chapter Eight, we'll talk about the Pitch-Treatment that will have a broader act breakdown strategy in a more narrative form using *Opportunity Knockout* as an example again.

*   *   *

In the end, as you navigate The Three Cs, you'll begin to see all the possibilities open up before you. If you write with a circular style, in other words, going back and forth between acts, adding or deleting stuff that works or doesn't, you'll get the story together a lot faster, and the overall structure will come together very nicely for you. The Three Cs *complete* your story.

If you're still having trouble figuring out how to break your acts, then see the *Solving Screenwriting Problems* in Chapter Nine for helpful tips.

May the wind be at your back whilst you sail The Three Cs!

And those winds have now led us to the rocky shores *of The Three Ss of Action and Dialogue.*

Chapter Seven: The Three Ss of Action and Dialogue

The Hallmarks of a Great Screenplay

Subtlety, Subtext, and Symbolism are the hallmarks of a great screenplay. Also, they're three of the hardest concepts to infuse into your script. As a writer, I find myself constantly struggling to balance wanting to explain everything in either action or dialogue or letting The Three Ss do it for me. When you've written a lot of prose, acquiring the skill to be more cryptic and suggestive, leaving the reader to get the idea, is very difficult because you have little space to work in. However, by that same token, when you capture the essence of what you're trying to say via The Three Ss of Acton and Dialogue, then you've *saved* yourself a lot of space and pages—and keeping the page count down is very important for new writers.

So let's take a closer look at The Three Ss and see what they're all about.

Subtlety

There's an old saying that goes: "Say what you mean, and mean what you say." Well, whoever wrote that wasn't talking about screenwriting. Being subtle makes the difference between looking like a seasoned professional and a rank amateur. Let's take a closer look at subtlety shall we?

The following examples have been simplified from true screenplay format for convenience (mine).

```
INT. RESTAURANT - NIGHT

Jack stares at Donna, nervously stirs his
drink, sweat beads down from his brow. He
fidgets in his seat. The look on Donna's face
is one of worry. Jack's right hand is buried
deep into his coat pocket. He looks around,
spots the waiter, tries to make eye contact
with him.
```

```
DONNA
Jack, are you alright?

JACK
Oh, I'm fine. I just wish I could get the
waiter to come over.

DONNA
Why?

JACK
No reason. I think that we need some drinks
that's all.

DONNA
You have one right in front of you.

JACK
(looks at his drink)
Oh yeah, I guess I do ... ha, ha.

DONNA
If there is anything that you'd like to prop
... I mean tell me about, I'm all ears.
```

So, from that little snippet what have you gathered? Well, I'll tell you. Jack is nervous because he is planning on asking Donna to marry him. She suspects that this is the case. Jack is looking for the waiter so he can order a bottle of Champagne. He most likely has a box in his coat pocket with an engagement ring inside.

Overall, this could be a playful and romantic scene to watch. However, it is also a bit on the long side and could benefit from being subtler. Here's how I would revise this to that effect.

```
INT. RESTAURANT - NIGHT
Jack fidgets in his seat, stares at Donna,
nervously stirs his drink. Jack's right hand
is buried deep into his coat pocket.

DONNA
Jack, are you alright?

JACK
Oh, I'm fine. Maybe we should order drinks?

DONNA
You have one right in front of you.
```

```
JACK
(looks at his drink)
Oh yeah, I guess I do ... Donna, I've got
something to prop ... talk to you about.

DONNA
I'm all ears.
```

Here, I took out half the description, since it was not necessary to describe every detail of Jack's appearance. Also, the bit with the waiter was not necessary. And by taking that out, I was also able to eliminate and shorten the lines of dialogue concerning the waiter. Those types of things are for the director and actors to add while on set. All that was needed here was to establish that Jack is nervous about proposing to his girlfriend. I could have trimmed this even further, but you also want to keep the story fun and interesting while being subtle.

Now for a real world (albeit a movie real world) example of subtlety.

M. Night Shyamalan's *Unbreakable* has wonderful scenes of subtlety flowing throughout. In fact, subtlety seems to be Mr. Shyamalan's signature style.

In *Unbreakable*, Bruce Willis' character, David Dunn, is a superhero—although he doesn't know that until nearly the end of the movie. David suspects something is radically different about him when he is the only survivor of a terrible train crash, coming out of it totally unscathed.

As David learns more about himself and what he means to the world, he is *subtly* steered to this revelation by the mysterious Mr. Elijah Price (a.k.a. Mr. Glass, David's eventual arch nemesis), played by the equally mysterious Samuel L. Jackson.

One scene in particular really hones in on this message: the weight-lifting scene. In this scene, David is down in his basement lifting weights with his eight-year-old son, Joseph. Owing to the testament that children are infinitely more perceptive than adults, Joseph *knows* his father is a superhero.

Down in the basement, David benches a huge load of weight. David, surprised, asks Joseph how much weight he put on the bar. Joseph replies, "Two hundred and fifty pounds." David is both shocked and intrigued. He tells Joseph to take some of the weight off. Joseph secretly adds more weight. David benches it and realizes what's happened. Then they add more weight, David benches that, and still they add more weight (and a few paint cans). David thrusts the weight up while Joseph moves away onto the stairs. When all is said and done, David realizes he's just benched 350 pounds! More than he's ever done in his whole life. This is an epiphany for David. Now he must come to terms with whom he might actually be. And all of this was done without a big brouhaha as you typically see in superhero origin stories.

This scene insightfully exudes subtlety. Shyamalan doesn't have David leaping tall buildings in a single bound, or stopping locomotives with his bare hands. No, David Dunn is the Everyman archetype that just so happens to have superhuman abilities. Talk about breaking the stereotype for the superhero!

Subtlety can be your friend when you're trying to make a point without having to resort to tired old clichés.

That being said, there are plenty of times when the story calls for being not-so-subtle. Action films are the best example. You wouldn't have a great Colosseum melee in *Gladiator* if the writer were trying to be subtle. Nor would you have a thrilling space battle at the end of *Star Wars* if subtlety were the goal. And even though James Bond's subtle charm is captivating to the ladies, the way he dispatches ex-Soviet operatives bent on taking over the world is anything but.

However, you can have subtlety and action at the same time. One of the best fight scenes that I've ever seen was in *The Bodyguard*. Here you have Kevin Costner playing ex-secret service agent turned bodyguard Frank Farmer. During the movie, Frank takes charge and rescues his rock-star client, Rachel Marron (Whitney Houston) from a crazed fan trying to kill her. In doing so, Frank has incurred the wrath of Rachel's long-time bodyguard, Tony (Mike Starr).

Tony shows up at Rachel's mansion while Frank is eating an apple. Tony attacks Frank. Though Tony is nearly twice Frank's size, Frank is a battle-hardened fully trained ex-secret service agent and clearly superior in hand-to-hand combat. Tony is no match for Frank. In fact, while Tony attacks, Frank does not throw one punch in defense. Rather he manages to get Tony to beat himself up by simply avoiding attack after attack from the big guy—all the while continuing to eat his apple.

In the end, a frustrated Tony picks up a knife and looks at Frank. Frank's expression is one of deadly consequences. Tony realizes that he had better put the knife down immediately. Tony drops the knife and motions to Frank that he gives up. Frank says to him, "I hope that we don't have to have this conversation ever again."

Those were the only words Frank ever says during the entire exchange. However, the subtlety Frank employs here in order to deal with Tony's foolishness speaks volumes. This scene is exceptionally well written, well directed, and well acted with a hint of *subtext* as nary a word is spoken.

Subtext

Next up is subtext. Lots of screenwriting books will go on at length about the value of subtext and describe many examples of such. Essentially with subtext, you are looking to *say one thing, and mean another*. This is easier said than done. For most writers, saying what your characters mean seems like the natural way of doing things. In fact, in real life, subtext is not as prevalent as you see in the movies. Unless you're a politician, salesman, con-artist, or any other profession that requires multiple meanings to the things you say, most of us rarely use subtext when we talk with one another.

Yet in the movies, subtext is a great way to get ideas across and save a lot of time. Here's an example of what I mean.

Back to Jack and Donna again.

```
INT. RESTAURANT - NIGHT
Jack takes a huge sip of his drink, pulls out
his right hand from his coat (empty-handed),
and reaches across the table. Donna, looking
slightly disappointed, clasps his hand.

JACK
Do you remember that movie about the
penguins?

DONNA
Yes?

JACK
Remember how they mate for life? Then when
they have a baby penguin the mother goes off
to fetch food while the daddy keeps the egg
warm?
```

```
DONNA
I do -- finally males taking responsibility
and committing to something for a change.

JACK
I agree. They wait and wait for their beloved
females to come home after a long hard
Antarctic winter. And I'm sure that when the
male penguin sees his female waddling up the
ice shelf towards him, he's the happiest
penguin on the continent.

DONNA
The female penguin must also be quite happy
to see her man ... er, male at home waiting
for him with their little egg -- all snug and
warm together.
```

Okay, so you can see that they're not really talking about penguins but themselves. The subtext here is that Jack is desperately trying to find a way to ask Donna to marry him but can't quite get up the courage to do it yet. Donna senses this and plays right along. She knows what's up and will give Jack some space—but only to a point—to do what he's fixing to do.

Now let's examine one of my favorite films that is simply brimming with subtext, *Star Trek II: The Wrath Of Khan*.

Though many people seemed to have had a hand in the screenplay (including *Star Trek's* creator, Gene Roddenberry), the final writing credit really should go to Nicholas Meyer who was also the director of the film. The story is an evolution of several stories happening at once, and their famous literary progenitors are often quoted throughout. For example:

Khan Noonien Singh: "To the last, I will grapple with thee... from Hell's heart, I stab at thee! For hate's sake, I spit my last breath at thee!" Quoted from Herman Melville's *Moby Dick*.

Admiral James T. Kirk: "It was the best of times, it was the worst of times." Quoted from Charles Dickens' *A Tale of Two Cities*.

Doctor Leonard McCoy: "According to myth, the Earth was created in six days." Paraphrasing from *The Holy Bible*.

Khan: "Revenge is a dish best served cold." Paraphrased from the French novel *Mathilde* by Marie Joseph Eugène Sue.

Khan: "He tasks me..." Another paraphrase from *Moby Dick*.

And so on.

Meyer uses this same technique of referring to literary works in the next *Star Trek* movie he directed, *Star Trek VI: The Undiscovered Country* (the title literally lifted from one of Hamlet's soliloquies about death in Shakespeare's *Hamlet*).

For your part as a newbie screenwriter, using classic literature as inspiration for your screenplays is certainly a fine idea; however, don't plagiarize—strive to be as original as possible.

Getting back to subtext in *Wrath Of Khan*, the literary quotes illustrated above have direct correlation to the events in the movie. When Khan says, "He tasks me. He tasks me and I shall have him! I'll chase him 'round the moons of Nibia and 'round the Antares Maelstrom and 'round Perdition's flames before I give him up!" Most of this was paraphrased from *Moby Dick*. It is just a shining example of Khan's obsession to destroy Kirk at all costs—including his followers, his newly acquired star ship, and his very life.

The "best of times" quote from Dickens is also sub-textual as Kirk refers to his life. He laments getting old but has had a great life as a starship captain. He also meets his son for the very first time during the course of the movie but then loses his best friend, Spock.

The final quote from *A Tale of Two Cities* that Kirk gives—"It's a far, far better thing I do than I have ever done before. A far better resting place that I go to than I have ever known," as Spock is laid to rest on The Genesis Planet (a name taken from the first book of *The Holy Bible*)—is a brilliant sentiment overflowing with sub-textual meaning.

For example, it could mean:

- Spock is laid to rest on a world where life was created from lifelessness—a foreshadowing of the next film where Spock is resurrected in *Star Trek III: The Search for Spock*.

- Spock's sacrifice will be remembered with honor, just like Sydney Carton's at the end of *A Tale of Two Cities*.

- Kirk has finally come to grips with his mortality and can let go of his regrets and fears of growing old. He even says that he feels young again.

All of this was said in one line of dialogue quoted from one of the world's most famous novels. That's subtext!

There are other original lines in this movie that say more than just the words. For example:

"The needs of the many outweigh the needs of the few." This is quoted several times during the film and has greater implications when Spock selflessly sacrifices his life to save the crew and the ship.

"And how we deal with death is at least as important as how we deal with life..." is a quote at the beginning of the film, which is later revisited as Kirk broods over the death of his friend. Kirks son, Dr. David Marcus (Merritt Butrick), reminds him of this before he reveals to Kirk that he knows he is Kirk's son. One life ends (Spock's death) another one begins (father and son newly acquainted).

"Admiral, if we go 'by the book,' like Lieutenant Saavik, hours could seem like days." This is Spock telling Kirk (for Khan's eavesdropping benefit) that the U.S.S. Enterprise is damaged almost beyond repair and they are out of the fight. However, what Spock is really telling Kirk is to "sit tight" and that they'll be ready for battle in a couple of hours. Total subtext galore here.

Wrath of Khan endures as one of the best (if not the best) *Star Trek* movies of all time. It has lasted for so long (since 1982) and will continue to do so because of the literary quality of its story and dialogue.

The film works on so many levels that even non-*Star Trek* fans can appreciate it. For example:

- It is an obsession tale, like *Moby Dick*
- It is a tale of sacrifice and loss, like *A Tale of Two Cities*
- It is a tale of wrath and revenge, like *Moby Dick* and *The Holy Bible*.
- It is a tale about mortality and growing old.
- It is a tale about the renewal of life.
- It is a tale told with passionate and intrinsic subtext.
- It is an old-fashioned sub-battle tale like *Das Boot* (released a year earlier).
- It is a story about friendship and loyalty.

- Finally, it is a *Star Trek* story at its best, embodying all of those qualities and more.

And one last word. *Star Trek II: Wrath of Khan* is full of symbolism, from The Genesis Planet, to Kirk's bifocals, to the separating transparent wall between Kirk and Spock in Engineering where Spock dies, to the books in Khan's habitat on Ceti Alpha V, to the literary references, etcetera; all of which, are the final hallmarks of great dialogue, action, and story telling in general.

Therefore, the final discussion of this chapter will be on symbolism.

Symbolism

All right, so I've got a marriage-proposal theme going on in this chapter—I might as well continue with it. How am I going to make a symbolic gesture that will work with this scene? There are a few ways I could do this, but I need to keep in mind that symbolism should also be somewhat subtle and relevant. Some types of symbols are peppered throughout a movie and are hard to catch, but when you do, you get a deeper understanding of the story and are more connected to it.

Some examples are:

- *Blade Runner* - Rick Deckard (Harrison Ford) is most likely a *replicant* (an artificial human). His eyes glow ever so slightly when standing behind Rachel (Sean Young) in one scene—a telltale sign of a replicant. The unicorn dream Deckard has (a unicorn is a fictional creature, like a replicant) and the old photographs on Deckard's piano are other replicant-related symbols.

- *Inglourious Basterds* - At the end, when Lieutenant Aldo Raine (Brad Pitt) carves the swastika into the forehead of Colonel Hans Landa (Chrisoph Waltz), he says, "This could very well be my masterpiece." What is really being said here is that this movie could be Quentin Tarantino's masterpiece. The whole scene is a symbol.

- *Miller's Crossing* - Every time Tom Reagan (Gabriel Byrne) takes off his hat, he's about to do something rash and primeval. When he has his hat on, he is thinking though his problems and being rational.

- *Casablanca* - After Rick receives the "Dear John" letter from Ilsa, the ink runs as rain pours on it, as if Ilsa's tears over leaving Rick are coming through the words.

- *Chinatown* - Sight and seeing symbols are rife throughout the film. Jake takes pictures of subjects he's hired to spy on. Eyeglasses are used as devices representing good (unbroken) or evil (broken). Windows and lights are symbolic of seeing or hiding the truth of the mysteries of the story.

- *Opportunity Knockout* - In my rom-com, when Alison is fully under the nefarious influence of The Book, she removes her glasses that she wore throughout the entire first act. When she abandons The Book and is back to her old ethical self, she wears her glasses again. She's seeing clearly now.

- The Book itself is also a symbol. It is a MacGuffin (explained in Chapter Nine) that stands in for the *biblical apple* or *knowledge,* which got mankind kicked out of paradise. Follow The Book's secrets and the same will happen to you!

Here's how symbolism might help Jack and Donna at this very important moment in their lives.

```
INT. RESTAURANT - NIGHT
Jack is at a loss for words. Donna seems
frustrated. Jack looks out of the window and
sees the snow falling outside. Is it
hopeless?

[Note: "Is it hopeless?" is an author's
intrusion". This technique should be used
very sparingly and only to add something
meaningful when describing the scene.]

A couple walks by. The man is pushing a
stroller with a very happy-looking toddler
trying to catch snowflakes on her tongue. The
woman playfully smiles to both her child and
husband.

Donna also watches this moment of happiness
through the window.
```

```
JACK
(turns to Donna)
Donna, I love you! I want to spend the rest
of my life with you. I want us to be like
those people out there.

Jack gets up, goes over to Donna, and kneels
before her. He reaches into his pocket and
pulls out a box. Opens it up, reveals a
gleaming diamond engagement ring.

Donna's eyes bug out of her head -- she
swoons.

Patrons at the nearby tables are also excited
as they watch the couple.

JACK
Will you marry me?

DONNA
It's about time!

They both burst out laughing together. Jack
places the ring on her hand. They rise and
kiss. The patrons applaud.
```

So as you can see, *symbolism* saved the day! Well, maybe it just inspired Jack to take the initiative and overcome his fear and self-consciousness (sound familiar?); to do what he had desired to do all along. Seeing the happy couple with the child was certainly a boost. At first, I used the snow to symbolize despair, as Jack might choke and Donna might get up and leave. But then I used the snow as a symbol for hope and happiness, as the child tries to catch the snowflakes on her tongue.

There you have it, another happy ending with the help of subtlety, subtext, and symbolism.

Now go forth and do likewise, and remember The Three Ss *saves* you time—a luxury you cannot afford when crafting a 90- to 120-page script.

Two More Ss: Stop Reading and Start Writing!

At this point, you may have noticed that I haven't been bugging you as much to get off your ass and write. That's because for the last three chapters it's been okay to take in what I have been saying about The Three Ps, Cs, and Ss.

But the goddamn vacation is over now. So *stop* reading and *start* writing again!

In the next chapter, you're gonna write—and write a lot. No more bullshit, no more excuses. Either you're a writer or a fucking pretender. The choice is yours.

Let's start with the treatment.

Chapter Eight: A THREE-Stage Approach to Writing that First Draft

Where to Begin?

Okay fellow screenwriters, I say "fellow" as by now you've been writing pages of notes (genre, logline, title, character archetypes and personalities); a map of the overall story structure and basic act breakdown concepts; and even whole scenes (regardless of proper screenplay formatting) such as the opening, end, and major turning points with lines of dialogues (including subtleties, subtexts, and symbolisms), all in preparation for the *big push*: the first draft!

It's time to start consolidating all of that into an actual screenplay.

We're going to do this in three stages.

1. The Pitch-Treatment
2. The First Ten Pages
3. The First Act

At this point, if you can get through each of these stages, you damn well should be able to write the entire first draft of your screenplay!

Now I'm not offering a magic bullet here—you still have to do the work. And either you have the talent or you don't. In order to find that out, you need to make the goddamn time to write, and write consistently. By now, you should have the vision that you can write, and you can see through to the end of your entire story. And, above all, you have the belief that you are a writer and can be a good one if you try.

If none of these things is true, then it is time for you to put this book down and never pick it up again. Furthermore, you need to find something else that you're truly passionate about that you can commit to and believe in, since writing isn't your bag.

But I'm guessing that since you've come this far, you're willing to give Nick's crazy no-bullshit screenwriting method a try and bang out a real screenplay.

There's nothing better than the feeling of creating *something from nothing* and holding the bound pages of your story in your hands. Nothing. Except love maybe. But you can certainly love writing *almost* as much as another human being. But that discussion is beyond the scope of this book.

No more *beating around the bush*. Here it goes...

The Pitch-Treatment

First you have a pitch (a combination of a logline and a brief synopsis of your story), and then you have a treatment (a three-to eight-page narrative synopsis of your script). If you combine the two, you have a pitch-treatment and a complete road map for your screenplay.

Here's what I tell my students at this point: "Write a three- to eight-page treatment of your story and frame it as if you're trying to sell it to me." In other words, unlike a traditional treatment that you may send to a producer in lieu of a script, which is a clear narrative of the screenplay; instead, you create a kind of *advertorial* for the script.

Start with the title, then the genre, logline, setup, the treatment (or synopsis) broken out by acts, and finally the tagline. Don't worry about the formatting right now; this is for your own edification. When you have opportunities to pitch your stories, then you'll formally write up your pitches-on-paper and one-sheets to bring with you (see Trottier's *The Screenwriter's Bible* and The Great American PitchFest's website, www.pitchfest.com, for more on these).

The following is an example of the pitch-treatment from my romantic comedy, *Opportunity Knockout*.

OPPORTUNITY KNOCKOUT

Genre:

A romantic comedy sprinkled with corporate intrigue.

Logline:

At the top of the dot-com bubble, two executive recruiters who work for rival firms fall in love while competing for a multi-million dollar contract.

Setup:

OPPORTUNITY KNOCKOUT is an edgy Boston-based romp that centers on MIKE O'CONNELL and ALISON ANGELINA. Mike is a savvy rising star in the executive recruiting world, doing whatever it takes to claw his way out of debt. Alison is also a dedicated "head-hunter," whose skeletons in her family's closet unexpectedly catch up with her. Mike works for the most ruthless and successful staffing firm in Boston, ProTek Human Powered Industries; Alison's firm (Athenaeum Resources Group) is the most ethical yet struggling. These two young professionals are brought together by an unusual twist of fate during a time of great prosperity and excess.

Act One:

When a bidding war starts over a coveted contract, Mike and Alison's companies compete like crazy in order to win. Alison's boss, JOE MCCASEY, and his son, JAMES MCCASEY, are like a father and brother to her; therefore, she desperately wants to help her company survive. Joe was a former friend of Alison's late father, Thomas Vincent Angelina, who turned out to be an unethical businessman. Though Alison loved her father, she makes it a point to be nothing like him professionally.

Meanwhile, Mike's company will use every *dirty trick in the book* to prevail.

Mike's unscrupulous and ruthless boss, LARRY HURTZ, entrusts him with an *actual* book of staffing scams—famously rumored to exist throughout the executive recruiting industry—to which Mike must use in order to help his company win the contract.

So what does Mike do? He goes drinking (taking The Book with him) at his favorite watering hole in Boston with his buddy BRIAN PANDOLINI—who loves telling stories about making tons of money job-hopping between dot-coms, getting signing bonuses, and partying on the corporate dime. At the same time, Alison is doing likewise with her smoking hot guy-crazy B-F-F STACEY GREENE.

Mike and Alison get drunk and end up running into each other for the first time while trying to catch the same cab. And though the sparks fly between the two, their stumbling around each other allows The Book to fall out of Mike's bag and into the taxi that Alison ends up taking home.

The driver helps Alison out of the cab and gives her The Book. She dismissively puts it into her bag and staggers up to her apartment. As she passes out on her bed, The Book falls out of her bag and lies beside her.

Mike, on the other hand, realizes The Book is missing and frantically searches for it. He can't find it. He's screwed!

The next day, Alison wakes up to see The Book and all of its wonders beckoning to her—about to change her life. End of Act One.

Act Two:

At first, Alison unwillingly uses The Book to help her company prevail over the competition. Also during this time, Mike and Alison begin a passionate relationship where neither knows what the other is up to—until it is too late.

Over time, Alison falls deeper and deeper under The Book's nefarious influence. She both hates what she's doing and yet cannot stop herself—like a junkie. It gives her a professional power and control over her life that she's never had before. She even gets Stacey a job at the biggest advertising agency in Boston, for which she is clearly not qualified.

And despite Alison's guilt over using The Book, she pulls off the biggest scam in the history of staffing scams, ultimately winning the contract for her company.

Upon losing the contract, Hurtz threatens to ruin Mike if he doesn't steal The Book back. Mike is shocked to find out that his beloved Alison is the one who has it. He's in a real dilemma, and whatever choice he makes it will cost him dearly.

Soon after, during a Red Sox game at Fenway Park (Alison is a big fan of the team), Mike and Alison share a personal and romantic moment together as one of the team knocks the ball out of the park. This leads them to her apartment where they're about to make love. While she's in the bathroom freshening up, Mike sees The Book! It is lying on her desk almost taunting him to take it. But he chooses his love for Alison over his obligation to his company and leaves it with her. A decision made with disastrous consequences.

A few days later as Mike confronts his boss, Hurtz is incensed, and not only does he fire Mike (and subsequently ruins his career) but also *drops the dime* on Alison.

At a big company celebration over the winning of the contact, the call comes in from the company lawyer that they are now under investigation for fraudulent hiring practices. Joe knows it was Alison. She breaks down and confesses, and is then escorted off the company premises.

At least Mike and Alison have each other right? Wrong! Alison returns The Book to Mike's former boss. He says to her, "Well as least you have a head on your shoulders, not like that jackass Mike O'Connell."

Alison is shocked to find out that Mike has been lying to her about the nature of their relationship. Furthermore, Hurtz sadistically reveals to Alison that her late father was the author of The Book. Alison is mortified by these revelations and hysterically runs out of Hurtz's gaudy McMansion.

She is royally pissed, seeks out Mike (who is playing hoops with Brian), and subsequently gives him the beat-down of his life as she dumps his ass.

By the end of the second act, the economy collapses and everyone is shit out of luck: Mike, Alison, Brian, and Stacey.

By a miracle, Joe manages to save his company and then promptly has a heart attack. Alison secretly visits him in the hospital and vows to set things right. End of Act Two.

Act Three:

At the beginning of Act Three, Alison is now working for the bad guys at ProTek. She is fixing to bring down the company, and inadvertently allies herself with Hurtz's vengeful mistress, LAURA.

Alison gets "the goods" on Hurtz and exposes his scams at a huge shareholder's meeting at one of Boston's finest hotels. She is ultimately forgiven by Joe and is brought back into the good-guy fold.

Mike does his bit to redeem himself by helping a former victim of his old company, DOUG VALENTINI, get the job of his dreams. Mike doesn't know that this guy is also a close friend of Alison's family and will be an important factor later on as Alison hears about Mike's good deeds and starts thinking about forgiving him.

At the very end, Mike learns from Stacey that Alison is still in love with him. He decides to win her back and storms her office looking for her. Security is called, and they chase Mike all throughout the office. He bobs, he weaves, and ultimately finds Alison. Bursting into a conference room (where Alison is giving a big presentation), he says to her, "Alison, I love you, and I've come for the job interview!"

Alison is surprised (as is the rest of the staff). She decides to play along. "What job interview Mike?"

"The job interview for being your boyfriend again."

"What makes you think you're qualified for the position?"

"Because of what I've lost, and what I've learned... I lost the most important thing in the world... the only thing that made my life worth living."

"Which was what?"

"You Alison. You."

Alison, as she rounds the conference table approaching him says, "Mike, I want to believe you, really I do, but I'm afraid I'm going to have to ask for references just to be sure."

Mike, dejected, replies, "Oh Alison, sadly I have none."

To which Alison replies, "No Mike you have one, Doug Valentini. He's an old friend of my family's. He vouched for you and his word is good enough for me. Congratulations Michael O'Connell, you knocked it out of the park. You're hired!"

They kiss and the movie ends.

Tagline:

Can love survive a thriving economy?

As you can see, this pitch-treatment is a lot less formal than an official movie treatment, yet it sounds like something that you could be rattling off vis`-a-vis´ to a producer at a meeting.

In the above example, I've also included bits of dialogue—all major revelations—not holding them off to the end. Not all of the subplots are depicted here but enough to get me going at least. This is for my benefit and as memorized, I can embellish it all I want to intrigue whomever I'm pitching it to.

Now it is your turn. Put this book down, get your butt to a computer, and bang out a three- to eight-page pitch-treatment of your story.

When you're done, find people to pitch it to—family, friends, strangers, co-workers, whomever! Throw your story at people and note their reactions—good or bad. Whatever their reactions are, it's all good. At this point, you don't have to memorize it since you'll tweak the story quite a bit before you sign off on that final draft.

The bottom line here is that if you can write a treatment to your story after everything that we've discussed, then you can take the next leap and write ten (and only ten) pages to your screenplay.

If you cannot do that, then don't bother coming back because I won't be here when you show up!

The First Ten Pages

So, I trust that you've written your pitch-treatment. If you haven't, then I'll give you one more chance to do so. Don't disappoint me.

Done? Great. Let's move on.

Now, for the first ten pages.

Syd Field, master screenwriting guru, once wrote this about the first ten pages: "You've got ten pages to grab or hook your reader, so you've got to set up your story immediately."

How true.

If you cannot hook your reader within the first ten pages, then you've got some serious rewriting to do.

Here are some examples of what should occur by page ten:

- A tragic accident, explosion, or horrendous act of nature occurs spurring the action of the story forward. *Star Trek VI: The Undiscovered Country* begins with the destruction of the Klingon moon Praxis. This precipitates a new era of cynical détente between the Federation and The Klingon Empire.

- All the main characters are introduced: protagonists and antagonists. In *Chinatown*, Noah Cross is introduced via a photograph with a description of the scene in the picture. This is an ingenious move because we don't see him in person for nearly an hour into the film, though his evil presence is most assuredly felt.

- A catalyst, however subtle, is set in motion. In *The Passion of the Christ*, Jesus is betrayed by Judas and arrested by The Romans. We all know what happens after that.

- Someone from the past comes back to town. In *Payback*, Porter (Mel Gibson) survives a double-cross (where he was shot and left for dead) and returns looking for some payback from the gang responsible.

- A daring escape is made. In *Star Wars*, R2-D2 and C-3PO narrowly escape from the clutches of the evil Galactic Empire. And though Princess Leia Organa is apprehended by the sinister Darth Vader, a dichotomy of events is set in motion for one of the greatest rescue stories in history.

- Nature violently erupts and alters the life of the protagonist forever. In *The Wizard of OZ*, Dorothy is swept up by a tornado that takes her to the fantastic land of OZ and on a quest to get back home. We all know what challenges she has to face in order to achieve her goal.

- One or more characters make a life-changing decision or commit a foolish mistake, or both. In *Juno*, Juno (a teenager) has unprotected sex with her guy friend and gets pregnant. What is she going to do now?

I could go on, but you get the point. Make it happen in the first ten pages. Here are some practical examples of what you can do:

- If your main character is leaving home for some exotic location and a crazy adventure, don't waste time watching him pack his bags and get on a plane. Drop him in the middle of the jungle. Now what's he gonna do?

- If you want to show how ruthless the criminals in your story are, have them pull off a violent bank job the moment the story opens. I'm sure you'll be able to top that later on.

- If you want lovers to get together in a romantic comedy, then show how miserable they are on their own. For example, the female lead is always a bride's maid and never a bride. The male lead's selfish non-committal girlfriend leaves him for a more well-off guy.

- Someone wins the lottery at the beginning.

- The ensemble cast is gathered to go on a suicide mission behind enemy lines.

- The beloved family pet dies followed by its owner.

Horace (Roman poet ca. 65 B.C.) put it best: *In medias res*, meaning "into mid-affairs" or, in the middle of the action.

Get on with it.

Everything that you need to know about the characters and the premise of the story should occur within the first ten pages (give or take a few). If you can set into motion the events that will follow starting here, then you've got a story that will hook the reader and not let them go.

Damn right.

Now bang out those ten pages and see me when you get back.

Oh, I forgot, since you're new to screen writing at this point, you might want to check out the *Solving Screenwriting Problems* in Chapter Nine to get tips on learning the ins and outs of screenplay formatting. You'll need that skill as you progress from the first ten pages to the first act and beyond. But don't let that distract you from writing those pages. Learn formatting as you go along, not instead!

Go... write.

The First Act

And finally we come to it: The First Act. This is it. If you can write the pitch-treatment and the first ten pages, then you can absolutely, positively, goddamn hands-down, no bullshit write the First Act of your script.

What needs to be said about the First Act? Oh, nothing big, except that your entire story hinges on making that first act work. This is make or break time. If your first act falls apart, chances are that you'll never get through Acts Two and Three.

However, if you've followed my advice well, then you know how your story is laid out and the subsequent acts are in the oven baking just fine.

You have *all* the pieces to put the entire story together, and once you bang out that first act, you can finish the whole goddamn screenplay.

Here's a tip to get you through the first act. Whatever you do, don't stop writing!

Simple, hah?

By now nothing should be standing in your way to get the next 15 to 20 pages done. Since you've already written ten of them, you are a third of the way there!

Here's another tip: set a deadline.

I had a producer ask me to send her the first act of my rom-com (in whatever shape it was) that I hadn't even written yet! I told her that I'd have it for her by the end of the week. That was on a Sunday, and by Friday, I delivered 30 rough-hewn pages but pages nonetheless.

I had all of the pieces put together that I've been ranting and raving about for many pages now. Blasting through 30 pages of script in five days was a fairly straightforward process. Not an easy one but doable.

Now I'm not giving you that kind of a deadline, but see what you can do within a month. That's approximately 30 days. That's one page a day, that's all. Do that and you will be an unstoppable writing machine!

So to inspire you further, let's look at some really great first acts and some really shitty first acts. These should give you an idea of what to shoot for and what to avoid.

Star Wars

- Opening line and scrawl appears on the screen to get the audience up to speed *in medias res*. This sets the *genre* quite nicely: science-fiction/fantasy. Along with the kick-ass *title* (the 1977 pre-trilogy version), the opening line (actually the *tagline*): "A long time ago, in a galaxy far, far, away..." works like a powerhouse *logline* that grips the audience from the get go.

- Quick battle occurs between the Rebel Blockade Runner and an Imperial Star Destroyer. The rebel ship is disabled and captured.

- R2-D2 and C-3PO are introduced (minor protagonists, but I'd argue they are actually plot devices—see Chapter Nine for an explanation). Imperial storm troopers board the ship and start killing the crew.

- Darth Vader (antagonist with a symbolic name meaning "dark father" voiced by James Earle Jones) is introduced. His purpose is made clear, and he is certainly without a doubt a badass.

- Princess Leia Organa (one of the major protagonists played by Carrie Fisher) is introduced dropping the plans for the Death Star into R2-D2, one of the early-on catalysts.

- The droids escape to Tatooine.

- Princess Leia is captured.

- The droids make it to the planet surface. They argue and separate (only to be reunited before the end of the first act). Both are captured by the Jawas.

- Vader briefly interrogates Leia. We learn her purpose and a bit more about the politics of this civilization.

- We meet Luke Skywalker (the next major protagonist played by Mark Hamill) languishing as a moisture farmer at his uncle and aunt's (Owen and Beru) farm, pining for a grander life of adventure. We learn a lot about his hopes and dreams here, which beautifully typifies *The Three Ps*.

- The droids come into Luke's possession.

- Later, Luke sees part of the message Leia recorded for Obi-Wan Kenobi (Sir Alec Guiness). This is another major catalyst that spurs Luke to action.

- Luke argues with his uncle at dinner about leaving this god-forsaken planet—as his friends have. Owen refuses Luke's request. Luke storms out. Owen tells Beru that he's afraid of Luke being just like his father. Luke stares into the setting twin suns lamenting his fate. This is a serious foreshadowing of both Luke and Vader's characters and a great use of *The Three Ss*.

• Later, Luke discovers that R2-D2 is missing and plans to set out looking for him in the morning.

• In the morning, Luke and C-3P0 head out into the desert. They find R2-D2. Luke is attacked by a Tusken Raider (a.k.a. The Sand People). Luke is knocked out. The Sand People are frightened away by Obi-Wan Kenobi. Luke rouses and Obi-Wan (a.k.a. Ben) greets him. They leave the area.

• Meanwhile at The Death Star, the Imperial generals argue about the growing rebellion and the power of the Empire's ultimate weapon. Vader reminds them that the ability to destroy a planet is insignificant next to the power of The Force—and gives a little demonstration much to a disbelieving General Motti's dismay. Also we meet the other major antagonist, Grand Moff Tarkin (played by the ever mercurial Peter Cushing). This is an important scene as we learn about how this universe works and see The Force in action (albeit The Darkside of The Force).

• In the next big scene, Ben tells Luke about his father (i.e., Darth Vader, but only the Anakin Skywalker part) and The Force, and gives him Anakin's lightsaber. And finally, the entire message from Princess Leia is revealed. We learn a lot about the past during the Old Republic days and how important Ben's character is. Some decisions are made. Ben implores Luke to join him. Luke refuses, for the moment.

• Back on The Death Star, we see Princess Leia being tortured to give up the location of the rebel base.

• The next day, Luke, Ben, and the droids show up at a trashed sandcrawler that belonged to the now dead Jawas—the same ones that sold the droids to Luke's uncle. Luke puts two and two together and drives like a bat out hell back to his homestead. He finds the place burned to the ground and his uncle and aunt right along with it. Luke's life has now irrevocably changed.

- Luke returns to Ben and the droids, and here is where he makes the one decision that will propel the story forward into cinematic history. He says, "I want to come with you to Alderaan. There's nothing here for me now. I want to learn the ways of the Force and become a Jedi like my father."

And that's how you do an Act One!

George Lucas really put it together here. All the setups are in place, all of the major characters are introduced (except for Han Solo and Chewbacca, but there are good reasons for holding on their entrances until Act Two), and the major *catalysts* of the story are set in motion.

By the end of the first act, *Stars Wars* is rolling along like a bullet train that has reached its top speed. The movie will take many turns and build to a heart-stopping climax by the end, culminating with the battle against The Death Star. All of this is based on what we've seen in the first act.

It is a first act like *Star Wars* that makes this movie so timeless and unforgettable over 30 years later.

Now for another enduring classic of a first act. This time, we'll look at *The Godfather*, a truly memorable movie with a near perfect screenplay.

- Opens up with Don Vito Corleone (Marlon Brando) holding counsel for patrons who are attending his daughter's wedding. The don cannot refuse a request on this day. We see that despite the fact that Don Corleone is a gangster, he's an honorable man. This is a great way to introduce the *genre*: drama set in an underworld crime family. The *kick-ass title* says it all, as it implies many things about the don's life and business.

- We meet all of the major protagonists (and the don's sons)—Sonny (James Caan), Michael (Al Pacino), adopted son Tom Hagen (Robert Duvall), Fredo (John Cazale)—and most of the minor characters from lieutenants to friends of the don.

- Michael tells his girlfriend Kay (Diane Keaton) the story of how the don made someone "an offer he couldn't refuse." He also says that this is his family but *not* him. That is a very important part of Michael's personality and certainly adheres to *The Three Ps*.

- We are introduced indirectly to the main antagonist, Virgil Sollozzo (Al Lettieri), via a referred-to phone call. Just like showing Noah Cross from *Chinatown* in a picture, alluding to the antagonist in the beginning can give them even more presence later on in the story.

- After the wedding, Tom meets with a movie producer to get Don Corleone's godson casted in a film. The producer (who thinks he's untouchable) refuses the don's request. The next morning, he wakes up with his prized horse's head in the bed. This horrifying image is a very *symbolic* way of demonstrating the power and reach of the Cosa Nostra. One of the symbolic meanings of the horse is virility, and having its severed head in an arrogant producer's bed is a sure symbol that he has just been emasculated. Consequently, the don's godson gets the part in the movie. Gee, I wonder why!

- Soon after, we meet Sollozzo in person. He wants the don's money and connections to back his push to market heroin in New York. The don refuses because drugs are too dishonorable and dangerous a business to get involved with for the Corleone family.

- That doesn't sit well with Sollozzo, so he carries out an assassination attempt on the don—throwing the family into chaos.

- Don Corleone is gunned down in public by page 32. A true first act climax.

Granted, one could argue that the first act actually ends around pages 49-51 when Michael declares that he is "now with his father" while thwarting another assassination attempt on the don at the hospital.

Personally, I like the former for the ending of the first act, as it really is the culmination of all the *catalysts* that will make Michael step up and take control of the family. Just as in *Chinatown's* Act One climax, "The corpse hits the floor."

On the other hand, however, a 50-page first act is not out of the realm of possibilities. But as a new writer, you're not given the luxury of taking too much license with the established trends and standards for modern-day screenwriting. So try to keep your first act within the guidelines, and as you become a writer with real clout, then you can start breaking the so-called rules.

The beauty of this first act, however, is that nearly half of it takes place at the wedding. This is an ingenious way to quickly and efficiently introduce all of the major characters by getting them in one place at the same time. The wedding also sets the period (late 1940s post World War II), genre (crime drama), and culture (a traditional Italian-American Cosa Nostra family) for the entire story.

Everything you need to know to carry you through the rest of the film is in Act One, from the don's lack of respect for his new son-in-law Carlos, to Sonny's famous temper, to Michael's love for Kay and his desire to keep her away from the family business, to the loyal and disloyal lieutenants of the don, to the start of the mob war, and to Michael's rise to power within the Corleone family (if you go with the longer version of Act One). It's all in the first act. The rest is cinematic history, which has endured for nearly 40 years, just like *Star Wars*.

Now it's your turn to rise to this standard. But before you do...

Here are a few examples of bad first acts to avoid.

Star Wars: The Phantom Menace has got to be the worst example of screenwriting in the history of film. Coming from the man who wrote a fabulous screenplay with *Star Wars* (despite a few minor flaws), George Lucas not only *phoned this one in,* he undid all of his great work and will never recover this once awe-inspiring story of his creation. Sure, he's richer than God, but that doesn't mean he's the damn good writer he once was. Not anymore in my opinion. And I'll never understand why.

What's wrong with *Phantom Menace*?

- There is absolutely no act structure whatsoever. Fancy Star-Wars-y signature camera dissolves and wipes do not delineate movie acts. And don't tell me that going from planet to planet indicates a new act because that ain't how it's done! Movie acts are

established by the flow of the story according to The
Three Cs. *Phantom Menace* has none of those.

• By the end of the first half of the movie, we still do
not know who the protagonist or antagonist is. Is it
Anakin (whom we don't see until 45 minutes into
the film)? Is it Qui Gon Jin (who embodies none of
the true Jedi moral and ethical codes)? Is it Queen
Amidala/Padmé or Obi-Wan Kenobi? Well, they do
absolutely nothing but putz around for almost the
entire movie! And is the bad guy (antagonist) Darth
Maul, Darth Sidious, Jabba the Hutt, Whatto, the
Trade Federation, etc.?

• What kind of a setup and catalyst for the entire rise
of The Galactic Empire is a simple trade blockade on
a bullshit planet (Naboo) that has almost nothing to
do with the rest of the galaxy?

• The Jedi Council do nothing in this movie but bitch
and moan about prophecies and the Sith.

• The Sith do nothing in this movie but bitch and
moan about the Jedi.

• The beef between the Jedi and the Sith is never, and I
mean never, explained. So what's the point? The Sith
wants revenge on the Jedi; but revenge for what? A
few stolen light sabers or one of those fuzzy little
Ewoks? Please.

• Child Anakin here is a throwaway character that has
nothing to do with his future Darth Vader self.
There's no indication that he has the potential to
become The Dark Lord of the Sith—or anything else
for that matter. He's just a whiny little boy.

• There are no discernable *Ps, Ss, or Cs* happening
throughout the entire movie.

• Though not in the first act (if there were one), the
worst possible transgression to the time-honored
traditions of screenwriting is committed here when
Lucas explains how The Force works via the Midi-
chlorians. What the fuck?! You never, and I mean
never, explain a MacGuffin or else you lose its total
impact on the story.

- And you know that the screenplay is bad when the audience of hardcore *Star Wars* fans (who have been waiting 16 years for this) come out of the theater not cheering but looking dreadfully let down.

George, what were you thinking?

When you cannot answer the fundamental question: What is this movie about? then that is when you have to chuck the story and start over again. If anyone can tell me what *Phantom Menace* was about (and do it in two minutes or less), then I'll rethink my position on this godawful script.

Here's another example of a terrible first act from the rom-com genre: *Valentine's Day*.

The rules of the rom-com state that you should generally have: boy meets girl, boy loses girl, boy gets girl back, right? Wrong, as far as this bullshit attempt at a *movie written by committee* is concerned.

I am frequently amazed at how many people get their hands in the till when crapping out a mainstream money maker with no thought whatsoever about plot, subplot, subtext, and symbolism. These feckless scripts have no meaning, no message, and no purpose other than to rake in the dough on opening weekend and then bomb afterwards—once the word gets out that it sucks.

Valentine's Day certainly falls into this category. The main draw of this flick was Ashton Kutcher and Taylor Swift, along with an A-list cast—which is why it got made in the first place. Actors have to work, right?

Here's the list of writers on this multi-plot roadkill:

- Story by, Katherine Fugate and Abby Kohn & Marc Silverstein (the *and* separates those who did not work together, while the *&* means those who did). Perhaps it was a good script initially but as more and more people got involved it definitely devolved into the lack-luster film that was ultimately released.

- Screenplay by, Katherine Fugate (means that she either did the final rewrite or is credited as doing the draft that was sold)

- Executive produced by, Samuel J. Brown, Michael Disco, and Diana Pokorny

- Associate produced by, Russell Hollander and Mark Kaufman

- Produced by, Mike Karz, Wayne Allan Rice, and Josie Rosen

All of the above producers had a hand in writing this film, whether they yanked out pages they didn't like and rewrote them themselves, or phoned in changes they wanted to see, or marked up pages of the script with their notes; it doesn't make any difference. There's feedback, and then there's writing by committee. This movie is the latter.

And then of course director Garry Marshall contributed his thoughts on the script. He must have been pulling the hair out of his head trying to reign in this beast of a screenplay. This is the guy who directed the timeless classic rom-com *Pretty Woman* back in the days when a good script was the *first* consideration.

The first act goes something like this:

Reed (Aston Kutcher) asks his girlfriend Morley (Jessica Alba) to marry him. She says *yes*. Later she breaks the engagement and leaves him. Oh well. No boy meets girl, or boy gets girl back—only boy loses girl.

But in the end (on the same day!), he hooks up with his longtime gal-pal buddy Julia (Jennifer Garner), so it all works out. Looks like he got over the woman he wanted to marry real fast now, didn't he?

Then there's Jason (Topher Grace) and Liz (Anne Hathaway). She moonlights as a phone sex worker, and he's a mid-Westerner who thinks his girlfriend is a supposed "normal" woman with a nice office job. When he finds out the truth, he breaks up with her. But in the end, he learns that when you love someone, you love their flaws as well. Hmm, so talking dirty on the phone for money is a flaw? Well, I know many guys who would love to get their girlfriends and wives to spice things up in the boudoir with a little racy banter. It's not like she's sleeping with these callers.

Anyway, there's a football star (Eric Dane) who wants to come out of the closet, a businessman (Bradley Cooper) on his way back to LA from overseas (who is the football star's lover), a mother (Julia Roberts) who's a captain in the army on her way back to see her son, and some stuff with a kid who's in love with his teacher (Garner).

Oh, and there's the obligatory older couple of veteran actors Hector Elizondo and Shirley MacLaine that are supposed to represent wisdom and maturity—and lend credibility to this floundering story. They're anything but, and their roles are the most throw-away in both their illustrious careers.

You also have Jessica Biel, Jamie Foxx, Queen Latifah, Patrick Dempsey, George Lopez, et al.

The cast list reads like a "Who's Who" in Hollywood.

The entire multi-plot story is so convoluted that even when the plots are connected at the end, none of it makes any goddamn sense!

There is absolutely no act structure as none of the characters go through anything resembling a catalyst, crisis, or corollary. None of the genre rules are applied. And in fact, the story is almost impossible to follow regardless of genre.

And since most of the audience was the teenie-boppers who went to this film to see Taylor Swift, I noticed more than a few scratching their heads coming out of the theater as to what the hell they just saw.

If you are going to write a multi-plot screenplay, then watch and read *Four Weddings and a Funeral*, *The Player*, *Hannah and Her Sisters*, or *Love Actually* and see how this style of story-telling is done right while retaining the Aristotelian unity of beginning, middle, and end.

In total, 12 fucking people wrote *Valentine's Day*! And you wonder why critics worldwide panned it, barely making back its enormous production budget. It is a washed-out plot with absolutely nothing to give the audience to hold on to and take with them out of the theater—other than bad reviews.

How did a mess of a screenplay like this get "green lit"? Beats the hell out of me.

It probably had to do with money and deals already in place long before the script was ever written! Money and marketing were solely behind this project. Nothing else. Nothing of value. This movie will *never* be remembered 30 years later like *Pretty Woman*, despite having Julia Roberts starring in both and the same goddamn director!

Now you're probably thinking that I'm unfairly picking on Katherine Fugate here, after all she is the creator of the award-winning Lifetime television series *Army Wives*. And to be fair, I was not present when she was developing, writing, and revising *Valentine's Day*. So I don't know all the details and reasons that went into the changes that were made on the script that was ultimately shot and released. All I know is what I saw, and it may not be representative of her best work.

Unfortunately, my guess is that *Valentine's Day* will most likely be forgotten in 20 years, contrary to *Pretty Woman*. However, hopefully Ms. Fugate will have more critical success with her next multi-plot project *New Year's Eve*.

So there you have it. If you can write the first act, you can write the whole fucking screenplay. No excuses. You can see through to the ending and know your path to get there. And along the way, you'll take some twists and turns on the road, all the while learning and honing your craft.

Writing is a never-ending learning experience. You cannot learn all you need to know to write a screenplay *before* you write a screenplay. You'll never get out of your own way and write!

You need to write and learn concurrently. Your first draft of your first screenplay will most likely *suck*. Yeah, suck!

Maybe it will be good, but I'm betting not. And that's okay. Because the most important thing is that you wrote something. And now you have a real script to rewrite and polish to a brilliant shine.

And after several drafts, you may have a great screenplay or the worst script ever written (that's the talent part that I can't help you with). Regardless, you've got more than what most people have. Instead of drinking in the bars with your friends wishing you were a writer, you are now a goddamn writer!

I'm proud of you and so should you be.

Holding a sheaf of papers bound by those shiny little brads is a truly rewarding experience in and of itself.

Whether or not you sell the thing is not important at this point. What is important is that you wrote something. You crafted a story from start to finish, created characters, gave them hopes and disappointments, wove an intricate tapestry of plot, captured the imagination of the reader, and proved to yourself that you're not a bullshit talker—you're a doer!

Where do you go from here?

Well, I won't leave you clueless. The next chapter of this book should help to answer that.

Chapter Nine: Where Do We Go from Here Now?

Solving Screenwriting Problems

Either during or after writing the first draft, you're going to encounter problems that will trip you up and maybe even grind you to a halt. Well, there are ways to overcome these roadblocks and get the writing back on track. What follows are simple suggestions that will help you out.

Read Screenplays that Are Similar in Tone and Style

The first thing that I suggest to my students when they are stuck trying to figure out how to structure their story is to read screenplays that are similar in tone and style.

What do I mean by that?

Simply put, you can read a screenplay that may not be in the same genre as the one you're trying to write, nor have a storyline that is similar to yours, yet when you consider the story, you may say to yourself, "That is how I want my script to flow."

For example, I wanted to write a World War II action movie but have it flow in a style similar to Christopher Nolan's *Batman Begins*. Surely these two stories were very different, but the tone (heavy handed filled with regrets and philosophical differences between Bruce Wayne/Batman and Ras Al Gul) and style (film noir-ish with plenty of action/adventure) of *Batman Begins* were exactly what I was looking for to model my screenplay after. Therefore, I read the script *while* I was writing *Montana*.

Reading screenplays in general will help you in many ways both directly and indirectly with your writing. You will learn how to tell certain aspects of your story with efficiency and style. You will also learn how to structure your stories to make them work in the long run. You'll learn more about cinema and how the great writers did it—better than taking any class on the subject. And finally, you'll learn the fine art of screenplay formatting that is the bane of every new screenwriter's existence.

Get Reader Feedback

When I have my students bang out their first drafts, I'll usually mercilessly mark it up, much to their chagrin. Then I tell them to read the comments but *do not* go back and fix the issues. I don't want them to become serial Revisers. I want them to be writers, so I encourage them to keep pushing forward to the end of their scripts—keeping in mind what I wrote.

This approach is good for new writers who belong or will belong to writers groups. Getting feedback from other writers, friends, family, spouse (my wife is my toughest critic, but I know she loves me) is a very important part of the writing process. No one writes in a vacuum.

And you need to grow a thick skin because most likely everyone (including your best friend) is going to tell you that your screenplay sucks. Face it, people want to find things wrong with your writing because they actually want to help you (though some for their own ego's sake, too). Bad reviews are a *good* thing.

One of my closest friends (whom I know loves me like a brother) called the first draft of my romantic comedy *pedestrian*! I was incensed. I couldn't believe it. But my best friend, Dan, talked some goddamn sense into me. He said, "There is obviously something in there that is bothering him. Your job is to find out what and address it. Your job is *not* to bitch and moan but to write. Period. I only want to hear about solutions, not problems."

How true, man!

So whatever stage you're at—treatment, first ten pages, first act, or first draft—get someone or some people to read it and hack it to bits. Take what you think is valuable in their criticisms, find solutions, and don't fucking stop writing!

Put Your Money Where Your Mouth Is

Nothing gets you more motivated to write than when *your own* money is on the line. Let's face it, if you've invested a few hundred or a thousand plus dollars into something, you're gonna get your money's worth. So why not apply that to your writing?

Sure, writing for the love of writing is a wonderful ideal. But if you're like me, you've gotta pay the bills. So money talks and bullshit walks.

If you knew that someone was paying you to write that friggin' screenplay, you'd see how driven you were to write it and you'd make the time, no matter what. Well, why should that be any different from your paying yourself?

For example, you've just dropped $500 bucks on attending The Great American PitchFest (www.pitchfest.com) held in Burbank California annually. You've also purchased your airline tickets for another five-hunny, and you've lined up your buddies who live out there to take you in while going to the conference. All this, plus you've undoubtedly got throw-around money on hand to cover your expenses while you're out there.

So now you're in it for over a grand; you don't think that you'll be writing your ass off from now until then?

When I did this back in 2009, I had already written five screenplays, though they were all first drafts. I took the worst of them and spent three months tuning it up to be something I could feel good about pitching to real Hollywood executives. Then I spent weeks preparing my pitches, creating one-sheets, and reading the late Blake Snyder's book, *Save the Cat!*. Sadly, he passed away about six weeks after I took his master class at the PitchFest. His entire performance and infectious enthusiasm not only helped me to bang out my romantic comedy, but also was the inspiration for running my own screenwriting workshops, writers groups, and writing this book.

A little financial investment can go a long way to motivating you to do greater things.

Therefore, my suggestion to you is find an event like the PitchFest, pay the money, observe the date because that is now your drop-dead date, and get the fuck writing. Unless you like pissing away your hard earned cash.

Write Circularly

Mentioned in Chapter Six, this technique has proven very helpful to me many times over.

Since you have in mind how your movie should end, why not write that part first before writing the beginning? Also, there is no real reason to start at the beginning and work your way through to the end, writing in a linear fashion. In fact, it would be better not to.

Since film is a visual (and sometimes three-dimensional) medium, so should your mindset be when writing for this form of entertainment.

Often times, I bounce around from the end to the middle to the beginning and many places in between. I'll write one scene that I know will be taking place around the mid-point of the story and then go back and thread in subplots, my Three Ss, and setups— all the way back to the beginning if need be. It's not that I'm rewriting, but more that when I've written scene twenty, I know how to write scene six. Or, that I need to add a line or two in scene six to jibe with scene twenty. Or, add a new scene seven to connect the two (even over the divide of many scenes).

This is a well-established process for revising your screenplay and is also extremely useful for the first draft. The important thing here is to keep all of it straight in your head. When you can do that, you're living and breathing your story, and that's when the veracity of it comes alive on the page.

Screenplay Roulette - A Different Approach to Revision

The next thing that I'm going to suggest will be an act of hubris that goes against every established method of screenplay writing and revising proselytized by the greats. You're damn right it does!

Here it goes. Write a first draft of your first screenplay, then drop it and start the next one the moment (and I mean the exact moment) you write FADE OUT. Do this in a completely different genre with a completely different story concept. And then do it for the next one, and the one after that.

Do this for at least four screenplays in total. That's probably about a year's worth of work with no final polished draft to send to producers et al.

Now why is this crazy-ass idea any good?

Because aside from the fact that you'll have four completed screenplays that you can now polish to perfection and be able to answer the producer's eternal question, "What else have you got?" you will have learned a shitload about screenwriting from the first script to the last.

When I had gone to the PitchFest, I had written five screenplays in total. Only one was ready for producers to look at. However, I was encouraged to pitch my idea for a rom-com, and it was well received. Everything that I had learned from all those first drafts gave me the experience to bang out a fully polished final draft of a romantic comedy in nine and a half weeks!

Not only did I have other scripts that I could pitch and have ready for producers to look at within a month's time, but I conquered all kinds of writing roadblocks that plague writers to no end. I was now able to write scripts with confidence—writing fast, writing lean. I had learned the craft and knew how to successfully execute it.

Sure, I could have gone back and done the revision thing with my very first script until it was so-called perfect, but that wouldn't have taught me nearly what I learned by playing Screenplay Roulette.

In my first script, I had massive problems with formatting, screenplay length, dialogue, and action. The next one went a little smoother, the next one hopefully one day will be my Citizen Kane, the next one was a two-part mini-series, and the last one (as of this writing) was the rom-com. By the time I got to the rom-com, I learned all of the methods discussed in this book on how to craft complete stories and pull off writing fully polished screenplays that stand up to Hollywood standards. And I can take all of those other screenplays and tune them up in a fraction of the time, just as I did for my second.

I won't lie to you, learning how to write professional-level screenplays takes years despite your talent. You can either go to school to do this (possibly spending ridiculous amounts of money) and maybe come out no better than when you began because you spend years being a bullshit writer. Or, you can write your ass off, learn along the way, refine and practice your art until you get it. And when you get it, you fucking got it baby!

The Maltese MacGuffin and the Plot Device

Sometimes your story needs an inexplicable component (real, supernatural, or both) that drives the story forward. This is a plot device". Done right, the plot device can be very fun to write (and watch) and useful to your screenplay—as long as you don't abuse it.

A *MacGuffin* (a term popularized by Alfred Hitchcock) like in *The Maltese Falcon* (the falcon itself) are wonderful plot devices because the choices the characters make in relation to it can be quite intriguing: murder, betrayal, sex with ulterior motives, blind greed and rage, and sometimes acts of nobility and self-sacrifice. Plenty of famous movies have used MacGuffins, like *Raiders of the Lost Ark* (the Ark of the Covenant), *Cloverfield* (the Cloverfield monster), *Lord of the Rings* (the Ring of Power), and *Star Wars* (The Force) to name a few. MacGuffins are great ways to get your story rolling. My rom-com uses the enigmatic book of staffing scams titled *Secrets of the Grand Masters*, and is commonly referred to in script as The Book. And it is this book that makes the characters in my screenplay choose to do crazy things (some bad, some good).

Other useful plot devices are *The Red Herring* (a device used to divert a reader's attention from the truth—this is good for mystery genre screenplays), *Deus ex Machina* (an improbable event used to resolve a story line—famous in Greek tragedies but still in use today, e.g., the angels in *Battlestar Galactica* 2003-2009), the *out of the blue* character that reveals an important piece of information and then is never heard from again, and the *techno-babble* miracle device (like *Star Trek's* transporter) that gets the protagonist out of a seemingly impossible jam.

What really killed the latter television versions of Star Trek for me in recent times was an over-use of the "techno-babble" miracle device. You can't hit the reset button every time you write yourself into a corner. Be a grown-up and write your own self out, for Christ's sake.

A an example of a good use of this type of plot device is the Delorian time machine from Back To the Future. Though using the time machine is what get's Marty McFly and Doc Brown into trouble, it doesn't bail them out in the end—they do that themselves and that's why the movie endures to this day.

If you use a plot device, use it sparingly and only to enhance the plot of your story. Never use the plot device in place of the characters' endeavors to achieve their goals and desires. Never use the plot device to neatly wrap up the complicated mess you made throughout your story—you can do that yourself thank you very much.

Say it Loud and Clear

This next one should be obvious, but I'm going to discuss it anyway.

Screenplay action should always be written in *the active voice* and *present tense*. Everything that you see on the screen is happening in real-time, so why would you write your screenplay as if the events had already happened? In novel writing, you use the past tense, but the screenplay is ostensibly happening in the here and now, so write that way.

Use the active voice and present tense for action but not necessarily for dialogue. When people are speaking to each other, they sometimes tell stories, sometimes talk about what's going, and sometimes muse about the future. Dialogue will be in whatever tense the context demands.

Action, however, is what is going to be seen on the screen. Here's an example:

Wrong

```
INT. MIKE'S BEDROOM - MORNING
Mike woke up, turned his alarm off, showered,
and went to work.
```

Correct

```
INT. MIKE'S BEDROOM - MORNING
Mike wakes to the clanging alarm. Gets out of
bed, heads for the shower.

EXT. OFFICE BUILDING - DAY
Mike, morning paper in hand, cuts across the
plaza.
```

If you find your action sounding or feeling wooden or thin, then you're probably not using the active voice or the present tense. Both will also help to reduce your page count by using fewer words, making your scripts more efficient and flow smoother.

Formatting As as a Second Language

The enigmatic language of screenplay formatting is by far one of the most frustrating parts of the entire screenwriting process.

What the hell were they thinking when they came up with this gobbledygook? Why can't you just write it out so people can understand it and be done with it?

Well, you have no choice in this matter. You have to learn the current industry standard for screenplay formatting. However, once you do, you will find that it is an exceptionally efficient way to write and present your story in a "written visual" style.

Like any other art, screenplay formatting has evolved over the decades. Elements that were in use 30 years ago are no longer acceptable, such as CUT TO:. And with the ever-increasing level of technological wonders that appear on film (such as the glorious 3-D of *Avatar*) the demands on the screenwriter to be up on these new conventions will be even greater.

So how do you learn this shit?

There are three ways I tell my students to try.

1. *Read Screenplays*. Not only does reading screenplays help you to overcome story problems (as described earlier), but it also helps you get used to the screenplay language and offers ideas on how to format your scripts.

    The more modern the scripts you read, the more you'll see what types of conventions are being used today. For example: the SERIES OF SHOTS and MONTAGE were good ways to speed up time for the audience, but now QUICK CUTS and QUICK IMAGES are being used as the "shaky cam" technique becomes more popular.

    Bear in mind, though, that most of the scripts that are commercially available are *shooting scripts*. You are not writing a shooting script, you are writing a *spec script* (on the "speculation" that you'll sell your screenplay and become an established writer). Shooting scripts have scene numbers, camera directions, and descriptions of shots and special effects. Spec scripts do not. Shooting scripts are generally longer than their spec script progenitors. Spec scripts are lean and mean with no time for flowery description, long monologues, and bullshit.

Know the difference and read the shooting scripts anyway.

2. *Get a Book on Formatting.* I'm going to plug David Trottier's *The Screenwriter's Bible,* here because it is a great resource for formatting and revising scripts.

   There are other books on the subject as well. Whatever one you choose, turn to the section on formatting, bookmark it, and *while* you're writing, refer to it constantly. Trust me, you'll learn when to use master scene headings (a.k.a. slug lines) versus secondary headings, how to use dual dialogue, write out a MONTAGE, and how to choose between CONTINUOUS and LATER. And a whole lot more about the screenplay format.

3. Use Final Draft (www.finaldraft.com), or Movie Magic Screenwriter (www.screenplay.com), or Celtx (www.celtx.com), or ScriptWright (www.indeliblink.com), etcetera. Screenwriting software is indispensable to the new writer for learning formatting. They take a lot of the burden off your hands, such as how many spaces to tab over for a character name versus their actual dialogue. The programs have tools to not only help you properly format your screenplays (such as script templates for film and television), but have great resources for revising your scripts (such as Final Draft's Scene View).

   With very little learning time, you can be writing your screenplays in the proper format using these applications. You'll spend way more time writing than formatting. And that's what's important here: writing, not frakking around with software pretending to write!

When to Hawk My Wares?

Though not directly related to story development, I figure that this question is going to come up, so I might as well answer it.

Here is the short list answer:

• Don't try to market your fully polished first script until you've written at least another one (polished or not) and preferably several others after that.

- Don't try to market your screenplay until you've had some experience dealing with Hollywood types. This means getting your ass out to Los Angeles, even for a writer's conference such as the PitchFest. There you will actually get a real sense of how the Hollywood system works. Being naïve will keep your screenplay from ever getting read, no matter how good it is.

- By that same token, don't up and move to LA unless you have a deal in-hand (real working screenwriters will tell you). And make damn sure it is what you really want to do. In this day and age, you can be a screenwriter and not *have* to live in LA, but it's going to be significantly harder. Do what you think is right for you and your family as long as you stay connected to where the action is in some way.

  Fortunately, the industry is beginning to change as more and more production companies, studios, and media distribution outlets are cropping up all over the country and abroad. In Massachusetts, the tax incentives have been so great for filming that nearly 40 projects have been shot and produced in The Bay State between 2007 and 2009. There are similar stats for Rhode Island, Illinois, Louisiana, Vancouver, and other locations outside of California.

  This is good news for the wannabe working writer as they learn how to ply their trade in different markets. Furthermore, the Internet helps to level the playing field. Between webisodes premiered on YouTube (www.youtube.com) and new web-based media channels such as Hulu (www.hulu.com), Fancast (www.fancast.com), and Crackle (www.crackle.com) to name a few, the old guarded film and television institutions are starting to crumble a bit—but there is still a ways to go before it becomes a free for all. That being said, you still have to write, write often, and write well.

- Learn how to pitch your screenplay in two minutes or less. This is by far one of the hardest parts of being a screenwriter. Regardless, you *have to* be able to present your story to others with the same passion and enthusiasm as you had when writing it.

If you can't get others psyched about your script, then you might as well put it up on the shelf and let it collect dust.

• Grow a thick skin and learn to take rejection with a smile. This will happen to you almost every time, and you cannot give up because of it! Learn to persevere.

Don't listen to the screenwriting magazines when they tell you that you have a "snow ball's chance in hell" of ever getting your script read, sold, or produced. Screw that! Get out and write! If you're any good, got balls of steel (ladies you too), and never give up, you'll see some desirable results.

The only way you can guarantee that you will fail is if you don't even try at all.

• Make contacts out in Hollywood. Either find friends out there, visiting them as much as your budget will allow, or use the social networking sites to make LA connections that will turn into useful friendships. Don't be shy about using people (even your friends) to help you make contacts in the entertainment industry. Just don't take advantage of your friendships, don't burn any bridges, and offer some kind of value to your friends in return.

• Attend classes and workshops, participate in writers groups (or start your own), and become a member of a film industry-related association (like the Rhode Island Film Collaborative [www.rifcfilms.com]). Being involved in this business in any way possible will keep you psyched and working on your projects. The worst thing to do is to "one-off" a screenplay and then let ennui distract you from ever writing again. Stay connected and stay involved.

• Read the entertainment industry trades such as *Script Magazine* (www.scriptmagazine.com), *Variety* (www.variety.com), or *Hollywood Insider* (www.hollywoodinsider.ew.com) to get valuable info and ideas, and a feel for the industry as a whole. You can also subscribe to their RSS (really simply subscription) feeds online as well.

- Get the current *Writers Market For Screenwriter's & Playwright's Market* (www.writersmarket.com) and *The Hollywood Creative Directory* (www.hcdonline.com). These books are the first line of attack when submitting your queries to entertainment executives.

- Read all kinds of books on screenwriting (not just this one). Whether you read McKee's grand tome *Story*, Snyder's uproarious *Cat Nation"* series, Trottier's omniscient screenwriter's bible, or anything in between, there is value in all approaches and you should take it all in.

  Besides, you're going to need to know how to write a query letter, create a one-sheet, and put together a marketing plan that goes beyond just writing the screenplay. These books will help you with that and more.

- Enter your screenplays in contests but not to win. Instead, you'd be doing it to get it read. If you win, great! That's a huge score in your column. However, your chances of winning are slim, but your chances of getting your story read by the right people are good.

  Most contests employ script readers or *story analysts* that work either independently or for production companies. These people are invariably the first line of defense you have to get through anyway to have your screenplay looked at by the people who hold the purse strings. Quarter finalist and semi-finalists do get called by interested parties and that is always a good first step to landing an agent, getting optioned, selling your script, or all of the above.

  Several contests to help get you started are:

  o The Nicholls Fellowship (www.oscars.org/awards/nicholl/index.html)

  o Script Magazine's Big Break Contest (www.finaldraft.com/products-and-services/big-break)

  o Scriptapalooza (www.scriptapalooza.com/index2.html)

- o   Script P.I.M.P. or Pipline Into Motion Pictures (www.scriptpimp.com).

- Get a coverage done on your screenplay. Though not directly related to the marketing of your script, coverages can be useful tools—especially if the story analyst praises your screenplay, your writing style, or both. You can use these endorsements in your query letters to help catch the attention of an executive or their assistants. Then you might boost your chances of getting the story read.

Coverages can be pricey and often times can be very blunt in regards to their opinion about your work. You have to take what they say with a grain of salt. Script readers read dozens of crappy screenplays a week and do not have the time to give your well-hewn and sublime work the reading (or two) it deserves. I had one done on *Opportunity Knockout* and the story analyst missed the fact that it was an edgy somewhat satirical romantic comedy—which was ultimately *my* fault. Therefore, instead of bitching and moaning about his criticisms, I took what he said objectively and tried to address his concerns, in a subsequent draft, to make a better story that was more accessible for him and future readers.

No complaining about problems, only find solutions!

Use a coverage, regardless of whether you're praised or not, as an opportunity to further refine your work. These readers do know what they're talking about for the most part, and their feedback can be very helpful. You just need to decide for yourself what to take from the experience and what to leave behind.

There are many ways in which you can get a coverage done. The first place to start looking is in the aforementioned trade magazines. Also, just do a search on the Internet for "script coverage" and you'll find what you're looking for.

- And finally, keep writing, motherfucker!

Chapter Ten: Final Thoughts—The Meaning of Writing for Life

Now for the MacGuffin part. The reason why I gave this book such an abrasive title instead of: THE JOY OF SCREENWRITING, or TOME: THE ESSENCE OF THE STORY, or GLORIOUS WORDSMITHING FOR THE SCREEN, or some other bullshit like that, is to harmlessly poke fun at all screenwriting methods, strategies, techniques, and voodoo magic. None of them can replace the only thing that means a damn: *writing*. That's it!

You've been bitchin' about writing that screenplay for years. Well now you have everything you need to do it. You don't need to spend another minute complaining about how difficult the process is, how you have to plot out every last detail to the nth degree on a bunch of index cards or in a 100-page treatment, that you don't have the time, or you're simply not ready to do it.

Fuck that!

Stop being a Bullshit Writer and write!

Time is going to fly by right under your nose and you'll be looking at another December 31st saying to yourself, "My New Year's resolution is to write that screenplay." And then the New Year arrives and you find that you're too busy and too distracted and too intimidated to write a goddamn thing.

Then the next year comes rolling around and the same thing happens.

Newsflash: You're Gonna Die!

Maybe not today, maybe not ten years from now. But someday, you're all done. Are you going to die with the regret of never having written that story that maybe, just maybe, could have made a great movie? Is that what you really want?

What kind of a writer do you want to be?

If you really have the vision and belief that you could be a great writer, then anything else you do with your life is a frakkin' waste of time. Sure, you may make a shitload of money being a hedge fund investor. But if you don't write the story that is nearest and dearest to your heart, chances are you're not doing yourself, your family, and the world in general any favors.

I want you to succeed. Just by reading this book, you can see how passionate I am about writing and about helping new writers to get writing. But I can't do the work for you. I won't!

I have, however, in these pages, told you how I overcame my fears and self-consciousness and started writing for real. My story may not be your story. My screenplays will not be your screenplays. But my love for writing can and will be the same love that you have to do likewise.

Here are some encouraging words from some of my favorite movies. These ought to get you motivated.

> *The Godfather*. Don Vito Corleone tells Johnny Fontane (as he's slapping him on the face), "You can act like a man! What's the matter with you? Is this how you turned out? A Hollywood...? That ah cries like a woman? What can I do?! What can I do?! What is that nonsense? Ridiculous."

The lesson here is pretty self-evident. Stop crying about doing something and do it. Oh, and ladies, I'm using "act like a man" here in the sense of being a grown-up for both men and women.

Ask yourself, who would you want watching your back? Don Corleone and his no-bullshit drive to succeed should serve as a great example of a person who overcomes incredible adversity to be become The Godfather. Don't kill anyone or run a criminal organization—simply follow his lead. What more could you want?

> *Glengarry Glen Ross*: Blake (Alec Baldwin) has some comforting words of wisdom for the sales staff, "Put that coffee down!! Coffee's for closers only... And you can't play in a man's game... A-B-C. A-always, B-be, C-closing. Always be closing! Always be closing!! A-I-D-A. Attention, interest, decision, action. Attention -- do I have your attention? Interest -- are you interested? I know you are because it's fuck or walk. You close or you hit the bricks! Decision -- have you made your decision for Christ?!! And action. A-I-D-A; get out there!!"

I couldn't agree more. A little harsh, I know, but really this is the only way to succeed in this game. You've gotta be bold, brash, and brazen. Fuck (or in this case: write) or walk, nothing else.

> Now as the megalomaniacal Charles Foster Kane from the uber-classic masterpiece *Citzen Kane* once said, "I am the publisher of the *Enquirer*. As such, it is my duty—I'll let you in on a little secret, it

> is also my pleasure—to see to it that decent, hard-working people of this city are not robbed blind by a group of money-mad pirates because, God help them, they have no one to look after their interests! I'll let you in on another little secret, Mr. Thatcher. I think I'm the man to do it."

Even though the older Kane met an inglorious end due to his own narcissism, the younger Kane was so full of *piss and vinegar* that you almost believe that he's on the level. Regardless, this passion to "be the one to do it," is what you need to fire you up inside. Can you be that person?

Everyone can use a little defiant and ambitious Charles Foster Kane in them. Never let anyone or any book tell you that you can't write and pursue your dreams. **This is your life, your vision, your belief, and your writing.**

> And finally from *The Empire Strikes Back*, Yoda" tells Luke Skywalker, "So certain are you. Always with you it cannot be done. Hear you nothing that I say… No! No different! Only different in your mind. You must unlearn what you have learned… No! Try not. Do. Or do not. There is no try."

And then Yoda shows Luke what's for and lifts the X-Wing fighter out of the bog using only The Force. And so should you lift that screenplay out of the bog in your head by using the force of your will, creativity, and courage.

So close this fucking book, cut the crap, and write that damn screenplay!

Get, it, done!

Glossary

Antagonist: The main opposition to the protagonist of a story. An antagonist need not necessarily be a person; it can be an artificial intelligence, nature gone awry, a wild predatory animal, an alien, etc. The salient point is that the antagonist's job is to make the protagonist's life a living hell.

Archetype: As in character archetype which is an original symbol or motif of a person in a story. Character archetypes are not cheesy stereotypes. The *unrequited lover* is a character archetype as opposed to the *nerdy loser* who can't get the time of day from the *bitchy hot chick*.

Bullshit Writer: One of five type of writers who do everything else but write. They are: The Reviser, The Planner, The Start-Stopper, The Thinker, and The Talker. Don't be one of these!

Fear and Self-consciousness: The two worst emotions that can totally thwart a writer's confidence in themselves to muster up their courage and write. You must get past these soul-crushing inhibitors in order to let your true creative self run free. No fear, no self-consciousness, period!

The First Act: The most important part of your screenplay. The first act represents the entire catalyst for the whole script. Everything should be set in motion by the end of the first act. If the first act is weak, then the entire screenplay will fall apart. Conversely, if it is strong, then you will be able to blow through the subsequent two acts. See Chapters Six and Eight for more on the first act. If you can write the first act, then you damn well can write the entire screenplay!

The First Ten Pages: Give or take a few, the first ten pages should have all of the necessary components of your story introduced to carry the entire breadth of your script. Elements such as the protagonists, antagonists, setting, pacing, tone, and initial catalysts should all be represented by page ten. If you can't hook your readers within the first ten pages they are never going to read the entire screenplay.

High-Concept: A nebulous Hollywood term for a story concept that yields a screenplay, and subsequently a film, with huge earning potential. Summer blockbusters and romantic comedies usually fall into this category but any genre can be "high-concept" as long as it can appeal to a broad audience.

Kick-ass Title: A title to your screenplay that not only whets the appetite for the reader to dig in and read but also complements your powerhouse logline for a one-two punch.

Opposition: One of the absolute cornerstones to any good story. Without opposition a screenplay cannot drive its plot forward. See *antagonist* for examples of various types of opposing forces to set your protagonists against.

Plot: The series of main or significant events in a story.

Plot Device: An inexplicable component (real, supernatural, or both) that drives the story forward. MacGuffins, Red Herrings, Deus ex Machina, the "out of the blue" character, and the *techno-babble* miracle device are all examples of plot devices. See Chapter Nine for more information on when and how to use plot devices. Just remember to use them sparingly!

The Pitch-Treatment: A three- to eight-page narrative synopsis of your script. This is a combination of a pitch (an attempt to generate interest in your story) and a treatment (a roadmap of your entire story). The pitch-treatment also includes the title, genre, logline, act structure, and tagline to help you write that first draft.

Powerhouse Logline: The one- or two-sentence blurb that powerfully sums up a screenplay story idea. This is kind of like the TV description of a movie but designed to attract the attention of a producer or agent, e.g., "A man-eating shark terrorizes a sleepy Cape Cod island" – *Jaws*. Good loglines have a sense of irony inherent in them.

Protagonist: The leading character or characters of a story. Often, the good guy(s) can be bad guys set against even worse guys.

Spec Script: A lean mean narrative script that flows like a raging river that is easy to read and sells itself to producers, agents, development executives, etcetera. Spec scripts differ from *shooting scripts* as they lack scene numbers, camera directions, and descriptions of shots and special effects. You are writing a spec script on the "speculation" that you will sell it or use it to sell yourself as a writer.

Shooting Script: A final version of a produced script (or one that is being used for filming) that contains elements such as scene numbers, camera directions, and descriptions of shots and special effects. Usually these types of scripts are the ones that are commercially available; however, you are *not* writing a shooting script, you are writing a *spec script*.

Stereotype: As in *character stereotype, i.e.,* an oversimplified image of a person in a story. Avoid cheesy or cliché character stereotypes at all costs! The Irish drunk, the greedy corporate magnate, the street walking hooker, the gansta rapper, the Italian mobster, etcetera, are poor shallow stereotypes. Don't throw in a Colombian drug dealer simply because you need a bad guy. Find a *character archetype* to create a great antagonist from.

Story Concept: The overarching design or purpose of a story, e.g., "Stranded alien must find a way home." "Man sees woman on a train and goes on a quest to find her."

Subplot: The secondary mini-story that either complements or contrasts the plot.

Tagline: The one-liner that you see on a movie marquee poster designed to stick in your head and get you to go see the film, e.g., "You'll never go in the water again! - *Jaws*"

Theme: An idea that recurs in or pervades a work of art or literature. In screenwriting this is referred to as the *controlling idea*, e.g., "Justice will prevail." "Love conquers all." Etcetera.

The Three Cs of Story Structure: *Catalyst, crisis,* and *corollary.* Catalyst—the first act of a screenplay (25 to 30 pages) where the equilibrium of the protagonist's world is totally disrupted, setting off all the action to follow. Crisis—the second longer act (55 to 65 pages) of a screenplay where all hell breaks loose as the protagonist desperately tries to right their world. Corollary—the third and final act (20 to 30 pages) of a screenplay where all the setups from the first two acts get paid off and the protagonist's world is set right yet changed forever.

The Three Ps of Character Development: *Past, problem,* and *panache.* Past—a character should have a deeply rich and fully developed past that is carefully alluded to throughout the story. Problem—a character should be facing a serious challenge to their world which drives their actions and decisions forward. Panache—a character should have a special or unique personality that sets them apart from mediocrity and makes them memorable.

The Three Ss of Action and Dialogue: *Subtlety, subtext,* and *symbolism*. Subtlety—in writing action or dialogue, keeping the flow of the scene short and sweet works better than inundating the reader with way too much description they don't need to understand what's going on. Subtext—is saying more with less by using superficial dialogue to make inferences to greater and deeper meanings thereby saving time on the page and screen. Symbolism–using iconic images, gestures, sounds, names, literary references, objects, or even whole scenes to exemplify greater and deeper meanings (like subtext) in your screenwriting.

"Writable" Story: A story that you as a writer can see through to the end and be able to write wholly and completely without fear of being tripped up by the usual writer's roadblocks: plot holes, dead-end story lines, contradictions, lackluster characters, etc.

Index

ABOUT THE AUTHOR

Nicholas "Nick" Iandolo is a screenwriter and author living in Dedham, MA... yadda, yadda, yadda. Screw that! Here's the real deal about me:

I am an over-caffeinated, Doors- and Pink Floyd-loving, craft brewed beer-drinking (read: Sam Adams), sci-fi geeking, movie-watching, opera-loving, Italian- and grilled food-cooking, schmoozing, mad-writing, over-the-top karaoke-singing, super dad and wacky husband!

Sure, I've worked in the corporate world for many years, have written a ridiculous amount of marketing and communications media, and have toed the company line longer than I care to admit.

But that ain't me any longer. You've read the goddamn book, you know what my writing is all about. And that's just the beginning, baby.

And what do you need to know about my life, huh? You've got your own shit to focus on. Now get back to your writing, or I'll come to your house and kick your ass!

With love,
Nick

Write me, blog with me, friend me, or link-in with me here:

nick@tenthsphere.com
www.tenthsphere.com
www.facebook.com/cutthecrapandwrite
www.linkedin.com/in/cutthecrapandwrite

Follow me on Twitter @cutcrapwrite

I'd love to hear what you think of this book, whether you find it totally helpful, or you think I'm full of shit and wanna tell me to "fuck off." Either way, I'm good. Peace.

Made in the USA
Lexington, KY
29 August 2011